# HOW WHY WHEN WHERE

Weekly Reader Books offers several exciting
card and activity programs. For information,
write to **WEEKLY READER BOOKS,** P.O. Box 16636,
Columbus, Ohio 43216.

This book is a presentation of Weekly Reader Books.
Weekly Reader Books offers book clubs for children
from preschool through high school. For Further
information write to: **Weekly Reader Books,**
4343 Equity Drive, Columbus, Ohio 43228.

Published by arrangement with
Grisewood & Dempsey Limited.
Weekly Reader is a federally registered
trademark of Field Publications.

First published in Great Britain in 1982
by Ward Lock Limited.

**Library of Congress Cataloging in Publication Data**

Hollyer, Belinda.
   How, why, when, where.

   Includes index.
   Summary: Answers questions on many subjects ranging
from the abacus, acorn, and adder to the x-ray, yoghurt,
and the zebra.
   1. Children's questions and answers. [1. Questions and
answers] I. Justice, Jennifer. II. Paton, John,
1914-      . III. Maclean, Colin, ill. IV. Maclean,
Moira, ill. V. Title.
AG195.H65  1984      031'.02      84-2837
ISBN  0-668-06159-6

Printed in Italy by Vallardi Industrie
Grafiche, Milan

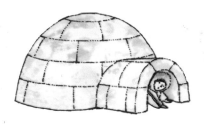

# HOW WHY WHEN WHERE

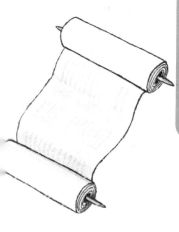

Belinda Hollyer

Jennifer Justice

John Paton

*Illustrated by*

Colin and Moira Maclean

**Weekly Reader Books**

# HOW IT HAPPENED LONG AGO

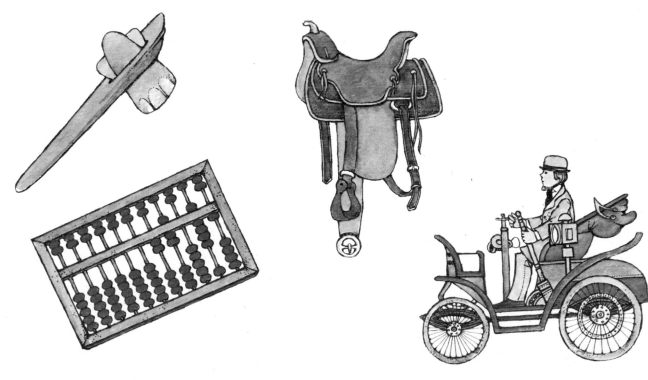

# People Who lived in Caves

## How did people live, thousands and thousands of years ago?

Thousands of years ago, people had no houses. These early people lived in caves. They hunted wild animals. The skins of the animals were used for clothes and they ate the meat. Sometimes they made tents of animal skins too.

The early people had no settled homes. They moved around, following herds of animals – animals such as reindeer, bison and huge, hairy mammoths.

## How did early people make their clothes?

They hunted animals with flint-tipped spears. When the skin was taken from the animals, they scraped the skin clean. Then they sewed the skins together with bone needles to make warm clothes. In the cold winters they probably wore clothes something like those eskimos wear today.

## What kind of tools and weapons did early people use?

These early people did not have any metals such as iron or bronze. They are called Stone Age people because they made their tools by chipping pieces of stone, usually flint. All sorts of shapes were produced, from big hand-axes to fine arrow heads.

They made necklaces and bracelets of bones and teeth.

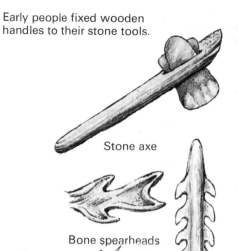

Early people fixed wooden handles to their stone tools.

Stone axe

Bone spear

Bone spearheads

# How Measuring Began

## What measurements were first used?

Long ago, people used their hands and arms for measuring things. The width of a first finger was called a *digit*. It was used to measure tiny things. The width of a palm was called a *handbreadth*, and the width of an outstretched hand was called a *span*. The distance between an elbow and the tip of the longest finger was also used. This was called a *cubit*.

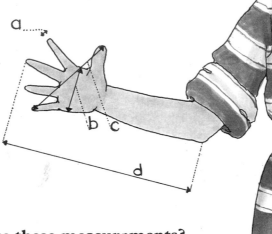

## How accurate were these measurements?

It is easy to see that there could be trouble with measurements like these. They would do if you wanted to know roughly how long something was, but they would not be good for exactness. The width of a hand, or the length of an arm, can be too different from person to person. So, in the end, people had to agree on a *standard measurement*.

## How were standard measurements made?

The cubit is a good example of how standards were invented. Everyone in a group of people agreed how long a cubit should be. They made a piece of metal, wood or clay the right length. This standard cubit was kept in a safe place, and people could check their idea of a cubit against the standard one.

Below: This man's arm and hand show how the measurements were made. You could try these on your own arm and hand. The bit marked *a* is the digit, and *b* is the hand-breadth. The span is *c*, and *d* is the cubit. How much do these measure on you?

8

Shekels

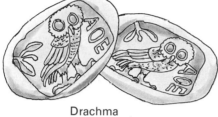
Drachma

## How else was land measured?

One way of measuring land that was an unusual one, happened in India. If someone wanted to buy land, coins were put around the edge of the piece of ground. All the coins touched each other. The cost of the land was said to be the number of coins it took to surround it!

For small pieces of land, the cubit measure could be used. A long piece of rope could be knotted for each cubit length, and then stretched along the edge of the land. You would have to count up the knots to find the length.

## How was distance measured?

The Romans invented a way of measuring distance that we still sometimes use today. The measurement was called a *mile*. A mile was a thousand footsteps. The Romans marked their miles with special stones called milestones. You can still see some milestones today on the edges of roads.

Many years after the Romans, another way of measuring distance was used. It was done with a chain, and farmers marked out the sides of their fields with this. Each link in the chain was the same length, so they could be sure that all the measurements were exact.

## How were coins used as measures?

The coins above are from the ancient world. People first used metal coins as weights, to find out how heavy things were. But the weights were not always the same, and some merchants cheated by having different ones. So new ones were made, that were exactly the same for everyone. In time, these metal weights were used as money. You could exchange them for food or clothes because their *value* had been agreed, and was the same everywhere.

The earliest coin-weights were lead. Later coins were made from gold or silver, or a mixture of these.

## How was land measured?

At first it was hard to work out how to measure large bits of land. This man is using a way that was invented in ancient times. Fields were measured by how much land could be ploughed by a pair of oxen in one day. This worked quite well!

# More About Measuring

## How could time be measured?

If you did not have a clock to tell you what the time was, how could you know? Many people in ancient lands tried to work out a good way of doing this. If you could see the Sun, you could work out the time from its position in the sky. But this was no help on a cloudy day, or at night. The pictures on the right show just some of the ways in which people tried to measure time.

Above: The sand clock on the left is still used today. The sand trickles slowly through the hole. Some people use sand clocks to time the cooking of an egg. The candle clock on the right is marked in hours. The candle burns down to each mark in just one hour.

## How could the Sun show the time?

The Egyptians used a shadow stick to tell what the time was. They stuck a stick into the ground. During the day the stick's shadow moved around, as the Sun changed position in the sky. The sun dial at the bottom of the page is a more modern version of a shadow stick.

Above: A water clock has a tiny hole, through which the water drips.

Below: Sun dial clocks are still used today, but they show only the sunny hours.

## How could the Moon show the time?

Long ago, people noticed that the Moon changed its shape during one month. It went from being round, to being thin and curved. People found that there was a full, round moon every 28 days. They used the Moon to mark off the months. This was the first sort of calendar.

## How could the stars help?

Some people in ancient times used the stars in the sky as well as the Sun and the Moon. The stars change their position in the sky at different times of the year. By watching these changes, and seeing how long they lasted, people worked out a yearly calendar for themselves.

## How did people count?

Our number system is based on counting to 10, but not everyone uses the same system. The number 10 is a useful one, but the pictures on this page show some other ways of counting. Which one do you think is the best? Can you invent a system for yourself? What number will you use?

Above: This prehistoric man is using pebbles to count his sheep. Every stone represents one of his flock of sheep.

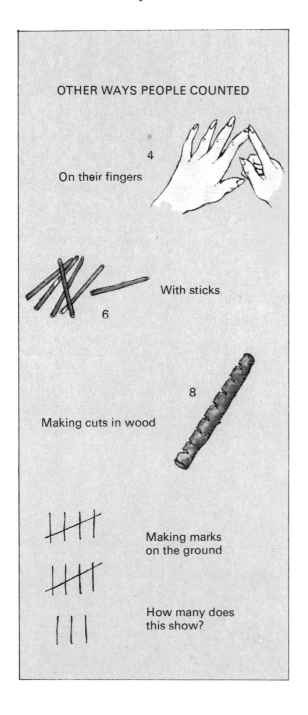

OTHER WAYS PEOPLE COUNTED

On their fingers
4

With sticks
6

Making cuts in wood
8

Making marks on the ground

How many does this show?

Above: The Inca people in America tied knots in ropes for measurement. Each knot was made for one thing.

Above: The Chinese used an *abacus* frame to count on. An abacus has rows of beads. Some people still use an abacus today. You can do division and multiplication sums on an abacus.

# How we Know About Ancient Times

## What are the ways of finding out about ancient times?

The people who lived in ancient times left all sorts of records of the lives they led. Some are written down in their *languages*, and some are found in the remains of their houses and cities. Even after thousands of years have passed we can use these records to work out what life was like in those times.

Today, specially-trained people study the records that are found. These people are called *archaeologists*. An archaeologist goes to the place where people lived in ancient times. The place is called a *site*. The site is cleared, and groups of people dig down carefully under the surface. With care and luck they will find all sorts of things from the past. Then the archaeologist uses these to work out how they were used.

## How do we know how old the records are?

When an archaeologist finds something at a site, the first question is "How old is it?" If the site has been used by many different people for thousands of years, the records will be found in layers under the surface. Something found near the surface will not be as old as something further down. So archaeologists have to be very careful to write down just where they find anything. If anyone else has dug in the same place, they may have moved things by mistake. All this has to be taken into account.

## What written records are found?

Some ancient peoples wrote on clay blocks, called *tablets*. Many of these have lasted until today. The writing tells us many things about life thousands of years ago. Other peoples used thick paper to write on. It would not last by itself, but some paper was put into clay jars. The jars saved the paper from crumbling away.

Right: A clay *tablet* with the *stylus* used to write on it. This writing was called *Cuneiform*. It was made up of marks, grouped in different ways. Each *pattern*, or group of marks stood for a sound.

Below: This sort of paper was made from reeds. It was rolled up into a *scroll* instead of being made into a book with pages. The scroll fitted into a clay jar with a lid. Some very famous scrolls, called The Dead Sea Scrolls, were found in jars like this one.

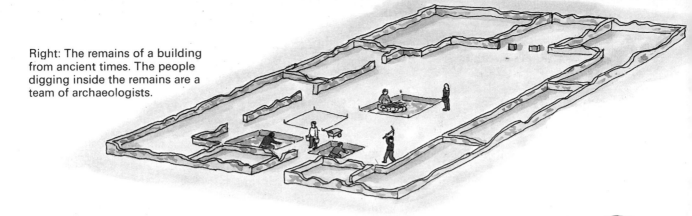

Right: The remains of a building from ancient times. The people digging inside the remains are a team of archaeologists.

## What sorts of things are found?

The pictures on the right show just a few of the things which have been found at ancient sites. Leather sandals sometimes last well in sandy ground, and the bone used for combs and hair pins does not rot. If pottery has been baked dry and hard it lasts well too, although it is usually found broken into pieces. The pieces have to be numbered as they are taken out of the ground. Then they are fitted together carefully, and any missing bits accounted for.

As well as these, archaeologists have often found tools and ornaments. The metal lasts well, even gold and silver. Floor tiles, coins and even scraps of clothing can also survive the years, and tell us many interesting things about the people who used them. They show what colours and patterns they liked, and what sort of lives they led.

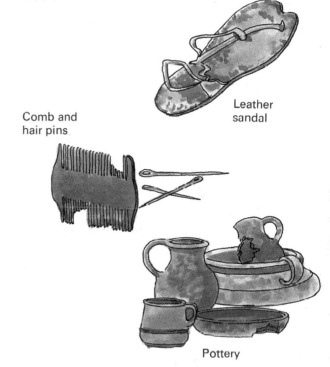

Leather sandal

Comb and hair pins

Pottery

Right: This is what the building above probably looked like when it was first built. Archaeologists can work this out from the remains of the building shown above.

# Life in Ancient Egypt

### What was Egypt's river called?

The River Nile is the long river that flows through Egypt to the sea. The land around the Nile, and at the place where it reaches the sea, is warm and good for farming. Without the River Nile, Egypt would never have been an important land in ancient times.

### Why did farmers settle around the Nile?

The rest of Egypt is dry and sandy, and farming there is almost impossible. But if the waters of the Nile could be controlled, farmers could grow many crops. The farmers learned how to control the river with dams and canals. These meant that the river's water could be used when there was no rainfall, to water the growing plants. The dams and canals kept the soil damp, when all other land was dry.

In time the farmers could grow more food than they needed for themselves. This was the beginning of the great Egyptian towns and cities, where some people's crafts could be *exchanged* for the food the farmers grew.

### What are the Egyptians famous for?

The most famous things are probably the pyramids – the enormous monuments to the Egyptian kings, called *Pharaohs*. The pyramids were amazing things to build, and the biggest of them were all built within one hundred years. To do that, about 25 million tonnes of limestone rock had to be moved and put into place, all by hand!

The Egyptians were also expert painters, sculptors and writers. Many of the things they made can still be seen today in museums.

### What was their life like?

Egyptians wore very simple, light clothes because their country was so hot. Linen and cotton were woven into skirts, shawls and tunics. Both men and women wore make-up, mostly around their eyes in heavy black lines. Their hair was sometimes dyed with *henna*, a red dye still used for this today around the world. Jewellery was used a great deal, and many rings, bracelets, necklaces, ear-rings and crowns have been found from those times. Music and hunting were very popular.

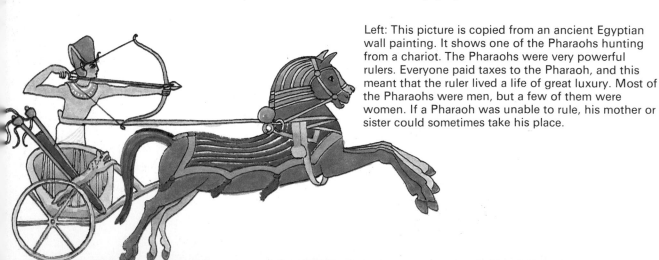

Left: This picture is copied from an ancient Egyptian wall painting. It shows one of the Pharaohs hunting from a chariot. The Pharaohs were very powerful rulers. Everyone paid taxes to the Pharaoh, and this meant that the ruler lived a life of great luxury. Most of the Pharaohs were men, but a few of them were women. If a Pharaoh was unable to rule, his mother or sister could sometimes take his place.

## What sorts of skills did the Egyptians know about?

It is not just the pyramids and the arts of music, painting and sculpture that the Egyptians were good at making. The ordinary work of crafts for everyday use was very advanced as well. Ancient Egypt lasted for thousands of years, and during that time many important tools were invented or improved, and many skills were used.

Some of these can be seen in the pictures on this page. Writing had been used in Egypt since the earliest times, and the man below is a special *scribe*. Not everyone could write. If you went to a scribe and told him what you needed to say in a letter or contract, the scribe would write it for you.

Because the land was mostly a clay soil, clay was used for making bricks, statues and tablets. It was also used by potters to make cups, plates and jars. The potter's wheel was used in Egypt at least four thousand years ago.

Spinning cotton

## How did the Egyptians make linen and cotton material?

The woman in the picture above is spinning cotton thread, using a special tool called a *drop spindle*. The spindle would be made from clay, and because it is heavy it pulls the *fibres* of the cotton out into a thin, even thread. Even today, drop spindles are used like this.

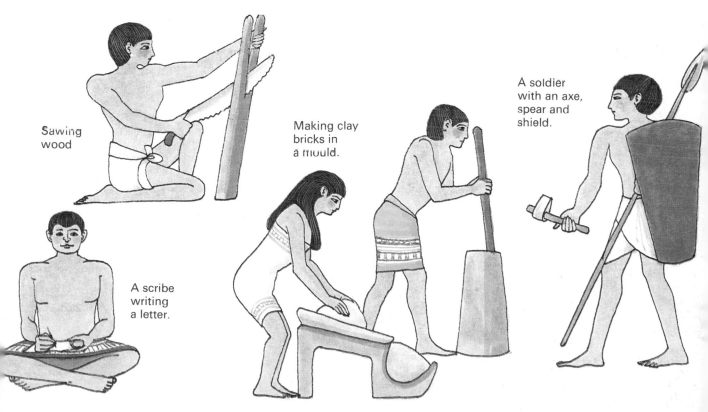

Sawing wood

A scribe writing a letter.

Making clay bricks in a mould.

A soldier with an axe, spear and shield.

15

# How the Pyramids were Built

## What are the Egyptian pyramids?

Pyramids are shaped like the buildings in the picture. They have four sides and come to a point at the top.

The people who lived in Egypt long, long ago built the pyramids as places where their kings and queens could be buried. The kings were called *pharaohs*. When a king died, his body was placed in a secret chamber deep inside a pyramid. This chamber was filled with treasures of gold and jewels. The way into the chamber was then sealed up.

## How did the ancient Egyptians build the pyramids?

The biggest pyramid of all is called the Great Pyramid. It still stands outside Cairo in Egypt, and many visitors come to marvel at its size. The Great Pyramid was built over 4000 years ago for a king called Khufu. When Christ was born it was already very ancient and mysterious. In it there are more than 2 million great stone blocks, each 2 metres high and weighing about $2\frac{1}{2}$ tonnes.

The ancient Egyptians had no machines. They had to do all the work with simple tools and the strength of many bodies.

Huge stone blocks were cut out of rock in several places. Some of these places were quite a long way from the pyramid being built. The blocks had to be put on rafts and ferried along the river Nile. Gangs of men dragged the blocks to the pyramid. There they were measured and cut to size. Then the heavy lumps of stone were dragged up a great sloping ramp. This ramp was built higher and higher as the pyramid grew taller. Then, when the pyramid was finished, the ramp was taken away.

The outer stones of the pyramid were white and polished. When the Great Pyramid was new it must have sparkled in the hot Egyptian sun.

# People of the Bible Lands

## Who were the people of the Bible lands? Where were these lands?

A large part of the Bible tells the stories of the Jewish people. These stories explain where the Jews came from and where they travelled to. This means that the Bible lands cover many different countries, from Egypt to Iran. All this is now called the Middle East.

## How did the Jewish people live?

You might know the story of Moses, who was an important Jewish leader. When Moses was born, the Jews were slaves in Egypt. Moses led the Jewish people out of slavery in Egypt. They spent many years living in the desert before Moses led them to their *Promised Land*, now called Israel.

## How did they live in the desert?

The desert was called Sinai, and people still live there today. There is not much rain, but a few plants grow which animals can eat. The Jewish people found life there very hard, for they were not used to searching for food and water. The picture below shows a group of them making their way to an *oasis*. An oasis is a water-hole in the desert. There they can rest and fill their water-carriers.

## How long did the Jews spend in the desert? How many of them were there?

The Jews spent about 40 years wandering through the desert, before they reached the Promised Land. The Bible says there were 600,000 men among the people. But today, many people think the real number was about 6000 people altogether.

## What was the most important thing for desert life?

The most important thing in a desert is always water. It is hard to find it in dry, sandy ground. There may not be an oasis close by. People who live in the desert have to dig wells for water, and the wells often have to be very deep. You can see the women above carrying water containers on their heads.

## What happened when they reached the Promised Land?

The Jews were divided into twelve groups, and each group lived in a different part. There were already people living in the land, and the Jews had to fight many battles with these people. At one stage the Jews were defeated. They were taken away as slaves to another land. But in the end, they returned to Israel. Their great cities had been destroyed, and the Jews had to start all over again to build their country.

## Who were the other people who lived in the Bible lands?

There were many groups of people there,

but one of the most famous was the group called the *Philistines*. It was the Philistine army who sent the giant, Goliath, to fight the shepherd boy from Israel called David. David beat Goliath, and grew up to be a famous king. Another group of people was called the *Canaanites*. These people had a god called Baal. The Jews thought Baal was a wicked god, and should not be worshipped.

A goat-skin was often used to carry water.

# People at Work in Bible Times

## What sort of work did people do?

Some of the most important work in Bible times was done by potters and metal-workers. This is because many people depended on their *products* every day. Pots and tools were used by everyone in lots of different ways.

## What did the potters make?

Some of the pots they made can be seen in the pictures on the right. The biggest ones were used to store important and expensive *liquids*, like oil, wine and water. People in Bible times did not use flat-bottomed jars for these liquids. Instead, the jars stood in special metal stands when they were not in use.

Important papers were also stored in jars the potters made. The jars protected the papers from damage and stopped them rotting. Small jars like the ones at the bottom were used to store herbs and spices, and also to keep scent and make-up in.

## How did the potters work?

You can see below that the potters used a wheel for their work. The brick ovens are *kilns*. The clay pots were baked in these until they were dry and hard enough to use.

Wine jar on a metal stand.

Jars for papers.

Small jars for herbs and spices.

Left: A potter and his assistant work at the potter's wheel. Another helper is filling a brick kiln with pots to be baked. This is called *firing*.

A metal worker with his helpers. The little boy is fanning the fire with *bellows*.

## What did metal-workers make?

Metal-workers turned slabs of different sorts of metal into tools and cooking pots that people could use in their homes. They made scythes and hoes for farmers to work with in the fields. And in time of war, the metal-workers also made weapons for the soldiers to fight with, and armour for them to wear.

Most metals, even soft ones, need to be heated before they can be made into different shapes. You can see the metal-workers doing that in the picture above. The fire in the background has to be kept going all the time. When the metal is ready for use, the workers hammer it into the right shapes. The metal might need to be heated many times before it is finished.

## What metals were used?

Different metals were used in those times, for different jobs. One of the most common metals was bronze. Bronze is a mixture of copper and tin, but it was better than just one of those by itself. Iron was also used for some jobs.

Metals like silver and gold have always been admired by people, but they are both very rare and very expensive. People in Bible times knew about these metals, but they were used only by very rich people. Gold and silver would not be any use as tools, because they are too soft. They would wear away quickly, and bend too easily. But some metal-workers made gold and silver ornaments and jewellery for special people. Sometimes this work had valuable jewels added to it as well.

Below: You can see from this market picture what sorts of pots and tools were made in Bible times. How many things can you see that we still use today?

## What sort of building work did people do in Bible times?

You can see some builders in the pictures on this page. Everything had to be done by hand, and so it all took much longer than work like this takes today. The carpenters are shaping pieces of wood. Wood was not used much in Bible lands, for it was rare and expensive. Brick and stone were used more often for buildings.

The brick-maker below is filling *moulds* with wet clay. These moulds will be left in the strong sun until the clay is dried hard. Then the bricks can be used for building. The man in the background is checking to see that the bricks are ready to use.

Stone masons were important people in Bible times. A lot of buildings were made from stone, and stone was also used for carvings and statues. The man in the front is using a *chisel* and a *hammer* to make marks in the stone. The marks will say what special things have been done by a king.

Carpenters

Brick-makers

Stone masons

Fishermen caught fish in the lakes and rivers.

## What other jobs were done?

The most important jobs of all were to do with making and gathering food. The fishermen in the picture above are catching fish with nets. Fish was an important food in Bible lands. The shepherds who looked after the goats and sheep in the hills guarded their flocks carefully. Their animals were the main meat that people ate. And the farmers who worked on the dry, stony lands produced grains like wheat and barley for people to eat.

## What special jobs were there?

Being a scribe was a very special job. Not many people could do that job, because not many people could read or write in those times. If you needed a letter written down, you had to pay a scribe to do it for you.

Music was something that people all enjoyed, and rich men like kings could pay musicians to play to them. The men below are playing a sort of small harp called a *lyre*. This instrument was popular in Bible times.

Scribes did all the writing.

Some people played musical instruments.

# Ancient China

## Who lived in Ancient China?

There were several different groups of people in China long ago, and they all lived very different lives. The leader of China was the Emperor, and he ruled over all the country. But China was also divided into a number of *provinces*, or parts, and each of these had a ruler as well. There were *merchants* who lived by trading goods, soldiers in the army, and *artisans* who made tools and ornaments. These groups were all very strictly separated.

The largest group of people in China in ancient times, just as in modern China, were the *peasants*. The produced the food on which everyone depended.

## How did the peasants live?

Peasants were important people, but their lives were very hard. They lived in tiny houses, often with just one room for a family, and worked long hours farming to produce food for the whole country. A large part of the crop went to the government of the province as a *tax*.

## Who lived in the cities?

The Emperor lived in the capital city, in a beautiful palace built just for him. The palace contained gardens and courtyards as well as many rooms, and it was surrounded by a high wall to keep it separate from the rest of the city.

Chinese cities were often very large, for everyone who worked at the day-to-day running of the country lived there. Different groups lived in special parts of the city.

Below: Some people in Ancient China, in traditional costumes.

An actor

Child

Woman

Man

## What was made in Ancient China?

Chinese art has been famous for thousands of years, and many beautiful ornaments as well as paintings, books and music have been made. Jade and bronze are two materials that were often used by craftsmen. Jade is a stone, which the Chinese called "the stone of heaven". It is very difficult to carve because it is very hard, and a jade object was a sign of great wealth and power. It was also thought to be magic.

Pottery has been made in China since the Stone Age, and the potter's wheel has been used for this for about four thousand years. Many of the glazes and decorations used in Ancient China were very beautiful and rare, and today such things are worth a fortune for collectors.

Above: Some of the things which were invented or made in Ancient China included jade and pottery ornaments, kites, fireworks and silk paintings.

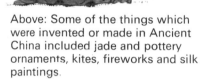

Chinese writing is done with a brush. It is read downwards.

## What sorts of things were written down?

Chinese is the oldest sort of writing in the world that is still used today, and in Ancient China many records were kept. The earliest sort of writing was done on bone, but later paper made from bamboo was used instead. The Chinese government kept records of orders and tax demands, while writers made up poems and stories, which were often illustrated by beautiful paintings. The first history book, and the first dictionary were made in China almost two thousand years ago. A special kind of hand-writing, called *calligraphy*, was developed. This was done with a brush instead of a pen, and it took lots of practise to do well.

# The Gods of Ancient Greece

## Who were the Greek gods?

The picture below shows some of the Greek gods, with their names and their main powers. The Greeks, like many other peoples in ancient times, belived that there were many different gods, and all should be *worshipped* and respected. Some religions today also have a group of gods, rather than just one god.

The main gods were Zeus and his brothers Poseidon and Hades. These three were in charge of the Earth, the sea and the underworld. The god of the underworld was Hades. He had power over everyone who was dead.

## Did the Greeks have female gods too?

There were lots of female gods, called goddesses. The main one was Hera, who was married to Zeus. Athene was the goddess of wisdom, and Artemis was the goddess of hunting.

## Where did the gods live?

The gods' home was on a mountain called Olympus, in northern Greece. But all the gods had magic powers, and they could travel anywhere in the world to see what was happening. The Greeks believed that their gods knew exactly what everyone was doing. If something was happening that the gods didn't like, they would use their powers to change it. Sometimes the gods sent messengers to people to tell them to behave better. They often punished bad people.

Zeus, god of sky and earth, and ruler of all the other gods.

Eros, god of love.

Apollo, god of music, art and light.

Poseidon, god of the seas.

Demeter, goddess of harvests and corn.

Hermes, the messenger of the gods.

Athene, goddess of wisdom and weaving.

### What sort of stories did the Greeks tell about their gods and goddesses?

The stories about the gods and goddesses were told to show people how they should behave. They said what the gods wanted from people, and how they should live their lives.

One story is about a giant called Atlas. He tried to fight the gods and their power. The gods punished Atlas by making him hold up the sky on his shoulders. Our word atlas, used for a book which shows maps of the sky and Earth, comes from his name.

### Did the gods always agree with each other?

The Greek gods and goddesses were not like perfect, magic people. They had good and bad sides, and often quarrelled with one another. When the people on Earth fought wars, the gods often took different sides in the battle and argued about who should win. In the famous Trojan war, some gods thought that the city of Troy should win. Other gods supported the Greeks, and sent magic powers for the Greek warriors. In the end, the Greeks and their gods won the war.

### How did the Greeks worship their gods?

The Greeks built temples for all their gods, and carved statues for them. The brought offerings of food and wine to the temples, and had priests who kept everything clean and tidy.

### What happened to the gods?

The Greek gods were important to the Greeks, but other people used their gods as well. The Roman gods are almost the same as the Greek ones, but they have different names. The Romans called Zeus *Jupiter*, and called Hades *Pluto*. Many stories are the same.

Above: Arachne wove such beautiful cloth that Athene, goddess of weaving, was jealous of her. Athene turned Arachne into a spider, and the Greeks say that is why spiders weave such clever webs!

Below: Pandora was given to mankind as a present from the gods. She was very beautiful, but she also brought a secret box with her. The box contained all the evil and wicked things in the world that make people unhappy.

# How Did People Live in Ancient Rome?

Life in the city was very pleasant for the rich people. *Aqueducts* brought fresh water from the mountains, and food arrived each morning from country farms. Many important people had beautiful houses, called *villas*. These were kept warm in winter with central heating under the floors. In summer, cool courtyards protected people from the hot winds.

Rich people also travelled in great comfort. Litters were small carriages, carried by slaves. Other Romans used horse-drawn chariots for their travel. Roman roads are still famous around the world. They lasted for centuries.

But not everyone who lived in Rome was rich. There were many poor people and lots of slaves as well. Their lives were not always very happy ones.

## Why did the Romans build temples?

The Romans built temples for their gods, just as we build churches today. The building on top of the hill is a temple to one of the Roman gods. There were many different gods, and each was important in a different way. Mars was the god of war, Ceres was the goddess of harvests, and Neptune was the god of the sea. Each god had his or her own temple.

A temple

A viaduct to carry water.

A villa

A litter

A chariot

The Romans built long straight roads.

## What was Rome's river used for?

The river that runs through Rome is called the Tiber. The ancient Romans did not use it for drinking, because it is dirty. But they did use it to turn watermills like the one on the left, and grind corn into flour for the people. Other kinds of mill were also used for this job. Bread and flour were very important, because most people depended on it for their daily food. There were about 300 mills in ancient Rome.

## What did Roman books look like?

Roman books did not look at all like the ones we have today. They were rolls of thick paper, sometimes tied up with ribbons or tapes. They were not printed by machines. People wrote them all out by hand. To read a book, you had to unroll it, bit by bit.

## Did ancient Rome have a navy? What did the ships look like?

The Roman army had a very large navy, and Rome was a very important sea power in the Mediterranean. They fought some very important battles at sea, and used their ships to attack other cities and countries as well.

Rome is not on the sea, but the river Tiber was wide and deep enough to carry some ships. Some of the Roman emperors put on mock sea battles with their ships on the river, to entertain people.

A ship like the one in the picture below, was used to carry grain and other food supplies. It travelled between Rome and other major cities on the coast.

# More About the Romans

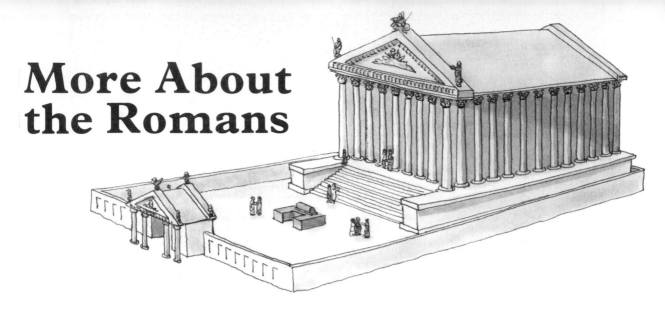

## Why were temples important to the Romans?

The Romans worshipped many gods, and each god had his or her own temple. Many of the temples were quite small. Only the priests or priestesses and their helpers were allowed inside. People usually gathered outside the temple to worship the god.

The Romans believed that their lives were guided by the gods. They hoped to bring themselves good fortune by pleasing them. So the temples were very important places. You can see one above.

There were temples to the Roman emperor too. It was the duty of everyone to worship him.

There were also temples to some foreign gods. The Romans borrowed many of their gods and goddesses from the Greeks. But they gave them new names. The Greek goddess of love, Aphrodite, became Venus. Hermes, the messenger of the gods, became Mercury to the Romans. Zeus, the king of the gods, and Hera, his wife, became Jupiter and Juno.

## What was a Roman villa like?

Only the wealthy Romans had villas. A villa was a big country house. Most of them were farms as well as homes. In the grounds round the house, workers produced enough food for all the people who lived and worked there.

Below you can see the villa itself. It had big airy rooms and was very comfortable.

## What is a mosaic?

A mosaic is a picture made from small pieces of coloured stone or glass. The pieces are pressed into soft plaster, which is left to harden. You can see a mosaic in the picture above.

Mosaics were used to decorate floors and walls. In ancient Rome, every villa and palace had mosaics. They often showed scenes from everyday life.

Mosaics were also used to make scenes of the life of Jesus, saints and angels in churches all over Greece and Italy.

## What is an aqueduct?

An aqueduct is a channel built to carry water from a lake to a town. The Romans were the greatest aqueduct builders of all time. You can see one below.

The Romans also built very good roads and bridges.

# Soldiers of Ancient Rome

**Who were the soldiers in the Roman army? What sorts of groups were they divided into?**

At first, all the Roman cities had to supply men for the army. Young men trained to be soldiers, in case they were needed. Then they all gathered together on special days, and the best were chosen to join up. Sometimes these men could stop being soldiers when the war was over. But later on, the army changed. Soldiers had to join up for 25 years, and they were paid enough money to live on.

The army was divided into *legions*. There were usually four legions, but sometimes in wartime there were many more than that. Each legion had smaller groups of soldiers who did different sorts of fighting. *Centurions*, like the one on the right, were in charge of a group of about 900 men. A centurion was a very important man.

**Who were the foot soldiers?**

Most soldiers in the army were foot soldiers. The work they did depended on what group they belonged to. Some built roads and bridges, to make it easier for the army to travel. Others fought in battles, or were used as a reserve to be called on if they were needed. But wherever they went, they had to march on foot. They did about 30 kilometres a day – or more if they were needed somewhere in a hurry. The foot soldiers on the right are dressed in armour, ready for battle.

**What was the cavalry?**

The Roman cavalry were the mounted soldiers, who rode into battle on horseback. Each legion had at least one group of cavalry. These soldiers wore special armour made from light metal *mail*, and they often carried javelins instead of swords.

Sometimes the cavalry rode without using bridles or saddles. The horses had to be specially trained for battles.

## What weapons did the Roman army use?

Many different kinds of weapons were used in battle. There were also special weapons to use if they wanted to break down city walls, or smash in heavy gates. The most famous of these was called a *tortoise*.

It needed about 27 men to form a tortoise. The men, carrying their shields, got into four rows. The front row held their shields in front of them, the men at the sides held theirs out to one side, and those at the back got in front of their shields. But the men in the middle rows put their shields over their heads, like the ones in the picture above. When the tortoise was ready, no spear or sword could get through the locked shields, and stones just bounced off the top. The tortoise could march right up to the walls or gates without being damaged.

Swords and javelins, like the ones on the right, were the most common weapons. The javelin was made from wood, with a metal "dart" fitted into a slot.

The soldiers below are all carrying javelins. The centurion in front has a sword and staff, while the soldier in a wolf skin holds the legion's special banner in front of the army, to lead them into battle.

# The Far-travelling Vikings

## Who were the Vikings?

The Vikings were sea pirates. They came from the countries of Norway, Denmark and Sweden, and settled in Greenland and Iceland as well. For more than two hundred years, the Vikings were the terror of the countries in the north. Their ships were feared, because the Vikings were such good raiders and fighters. Later, Vikings settled in many of these countries and stopped being pirates.

## How did Vikings live?

The pictures on the right show Viking people at home. Most of them lived together in large houses when they were not at sea. Their lands were hard to farm, and many of them relied on fish for food. They were famous for their bravery in battle, and for their songs and stories. Their ships were the best in the world, and the Vikings were excellent sailors.

A Viking house: everyone lived together in the long cold winter months.

Below: Viking ships were called longboats. They could be rowed as well as sailed with the wind. The *prow*, or front, of the longboat was carved with decorations.

A Viking settlement: you can see the different jobs that everyone did.

Building a hut

Making clay pots

Making weapons

# Knights in Armour

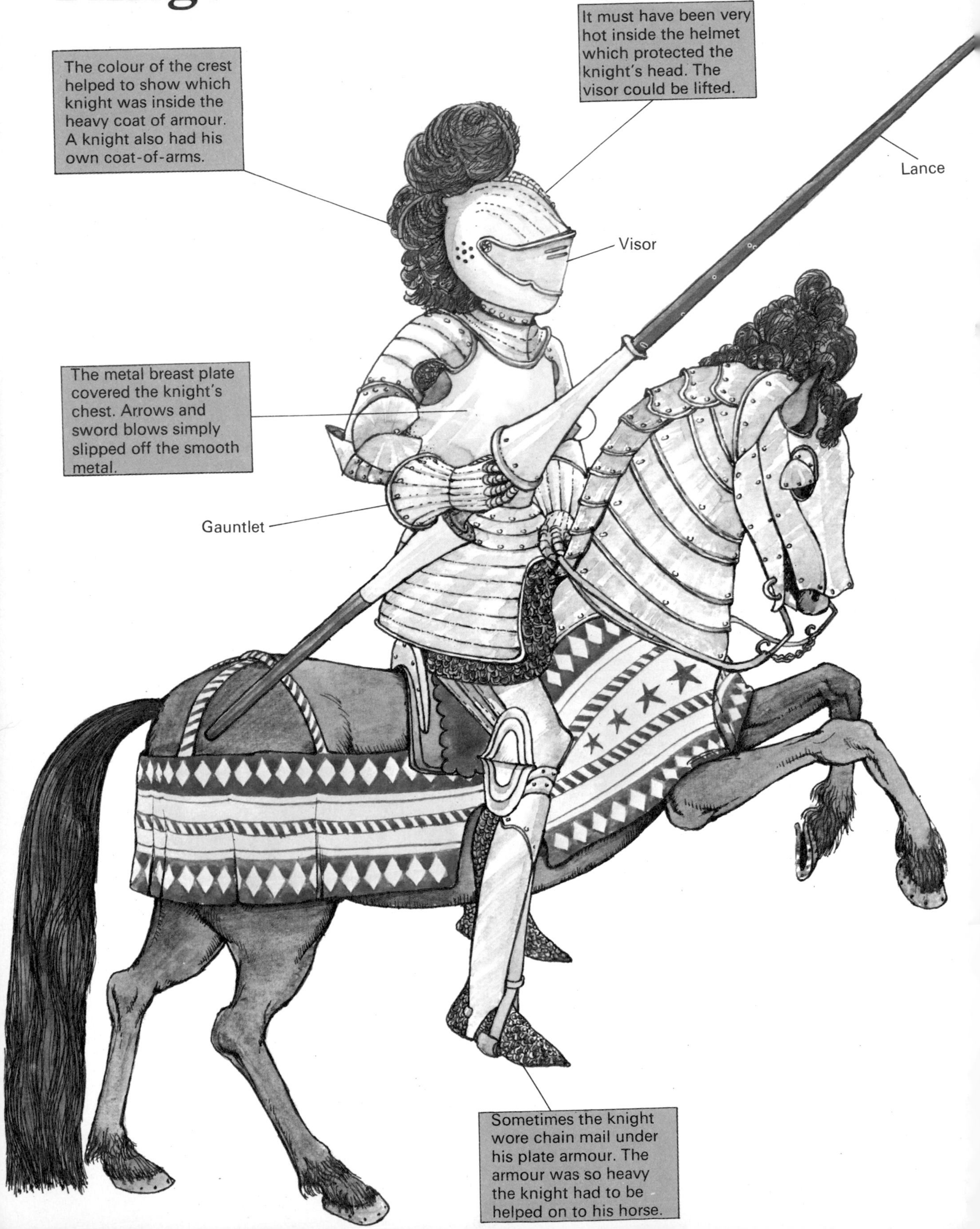

It must have been very
hot inside the helmet
which protected the
knight's head. The
visor could be lifted.

The colour of the crest
helped to show which
knight was inside the
heavy coat of armour.
A knight also had his
own coat-of-arms.

Lance

Visor

The metal breast plate
covered the knight's
chest. Arrows and
sword blows simply
slipped off the smooth
metal.

Gauntlet

Sometimes the knight
wore chain mail under
his plate armour. The
armour was so heavy
the knight had to be
helped on to his horse.

## How did a boy become a knight?

During the Middle Ages there were many kings in Europe. The kings often went to war against each other. Then they needed the help of their knights on horseback.

As well as being good soldiers, knights were also expected to be noble and kind.

A nobleman's son had to train for years before he could become a knight. First he had to work as a *page* in the castle of a baron. Pages waited on the ladies and learned to ride, hunt and fight. Then the young man became a *squire* to a knight. The squire looked after the knight's armour, and the knight taught him to fight with a sword and use a lance.

When the young squire reached the age of twenty-one he became a knight.

## What armour did knights wear?

Knights wore armour to protect them in battle. In early times they wore *chain mail*. This was made of hundreds of small metal rings all joined together as you can see in the picture below.

Then knights began to wear armour made of sheets of iron or steel. These metal plates were shaped to fit different parts of their bodies. The knight's horse wore armour too.

On the right you can see some of the weapons used in those times.

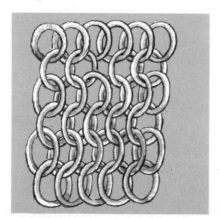

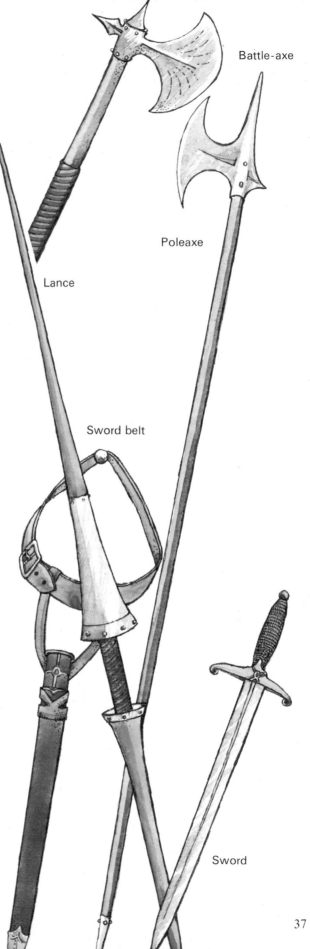

Battle-axe

Poleaxe

Lance

Sword belt

Sword

Scabbard

37

# How They Lived in Castles

**What was it like to live in an old castle?**

A castle was the strong home of a lord. It was built to protect the lord's lands and to defend his family and followers from attack.

The lord and his family lived in the high building in the centre. It was called the *keep*. The keep had very thick walls with narrow slits through which arrows could be shot.

The keep stood in the *inner bailey*. This courtyard had the kitchen and other store rooms.

The *outer bailey* had stables and gardens, and it was surrounded by high, thick walls with towers for soldiers. Outside, a deep *moat* ran all the way round the castle.

On the opposite page you can see inside a keep.

Keep

Inner bailey

Outer bailey

Gatehouses

The portcullis could be raised and lowered.

Well

Moat

The solar was the lord's own room. It was the grandest room in the whole castle.

The lord and his family ate and lived in the Great Hall. Here too they listened to minstrels and played games.

Soldiers guarded the battlements.

The people prayed in the chapel.

Sleeping rooms

Armoury

Spiral staircase

Well

People had to climb these stairs to get in.

Prisoners were kept in the dungeons.

# Farming Long Ago

## What was farming like in the past?

Farming was slow and hard, because there were no machines to help do the work. Everything had to be done by hand, or by animals. The tools people used were not as useful as the ones we have today. You can see how the land was ploughed, seeds sown and the crops harvested from these pictures.

## Who did the work?

At busy times in the year everyone had to help with the farm work. It could not have been finished otherwise. So the whole family, and anyone else around, worked in the fields at harvest-time. Any other tasks had to wait till that was over. Until the harvest was in, no one was sure they had enough food to live through the winter.

## What happened to the harvest?

The grains, like wheat and corn, were taken to a mill and ground into flour. Most people depended on flour for their food. If they had enough grain to sell some and buy other food as well, it was a good harvest. The mill in the picture above is a windmill. Wind made the wheel turn to grind the grain into flour.

## What happened after the harvest?

If it had been a good harvest with lots of grain, everyone was happy. The work had been tiring, but they knew they had enough food for the winter. So they often had a party, called a "harvest home" party. They relaxed with their family and friends, drank beer or wine, and ate lots of food to celebrate.

# What they Ate Long Ago

## What did people eat in the Middle Ages?

People in the Middle Ages did not eat as many different foods as we do today. Many things, like tomatoes and potatoes, had not yet been brought to Europe by explorers. Other foods could only be eaten when they were harvested. It was very hard to store food and eat it later. Meat could be salted, and sugar was used to *preserve* fruit, but both salt and sugar were very expensive then. So many people ate food we would think very boring. Most days, the poorer people just ate a sort of porridge made from rye or wheat. They might be able to have brown bread, a little cheese, and perhaps some root vegetables. They drank water or beer.

Rich people, however, ate more interesting food. The picture below shows a whole swan and a peacock being served to a lord and his ladies. These birds would be plucked and cooked, and then decorated with their feathers before serving. Rich people could afford to eat a lot of meat, but the poor only ate it on special feast days, such as Christmas and Easter.

The rich also drank wine, and ate expensive fruit like grapes and oranges. Their bread was white instead of brown.

## What was eaten at a Victorian banquet?

A banquet is a very special kind of dinner party. Some people still have banquets today, but they were very popular a hundred years ago. At a banquet, the table was set with a beautiful cloth, sparkling plates and glasses, and many different sorts of food. There were always flowers on the table too, and sometimes statues as well. It all looked very splendid.

Sometimes the table would be set with many different sorts of food. Many meals were different in those days. Food was not always served in separate courses, with sweet things following after savoury ones. Everything might be put on to the table at once, and the people sitting around the table could be served with little bits of many dishes at once.

When there were separate courses, banquets often had nine or ten of them! Now most meals we eat have two or three courses, but a hundred years ago rich people ate a lot more food than we do. They often ate meat and drank beer for breakfast, and then settled down to an enormous dinner sometime early in the afternoon. Do you think you could eat a meal as big as this one?

Oranges

Cherries

Cakes and pies

Tarts

Turkey

Carrots

Artichokes

Game pie

Cauliflower

Onions

Fish

43

# Inside an Old Fighting Ship

## What was a galleon?

A galleon was an old kind of sailing ship specially built for battle. It had three masts which carried lots of sails. And it had plenty of heavy guns that could be fired through holes in the ship's sides. You can see the *gunports* in the picture below. When the ship was not fighting, the gunports could be closed.

## Where did the crew live?

Life was very rough for sailors in the days of the galleon. Some of the sailors slept in the *forecastle* – the piece that sticks up at the front of the ship. The front of a ship is called the *bow* or *stem*. Most of the crew slept in hammocks slung on the gundeck. Some even had to sleep in the deck below. There was no light there, and it was very smelly.

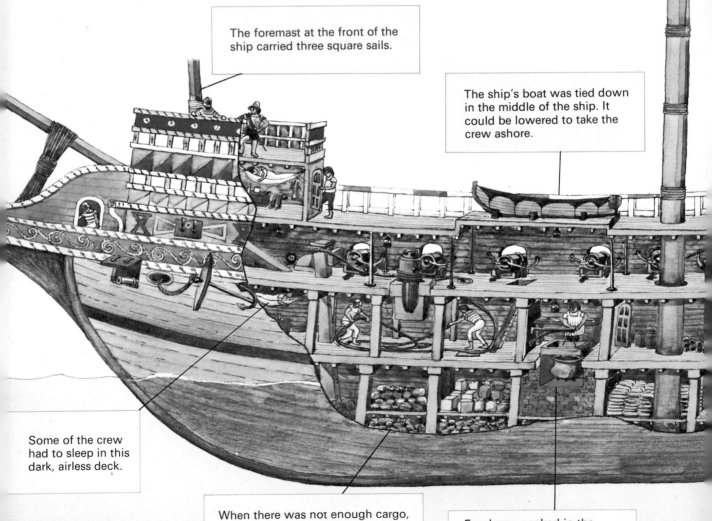

The mainmast in the centre of the ship was the tallest mast. It carried three big square sails.

The foremast at the front of the ship carried three square sails.

The ship's boat was tied down in the middle of the ship. It could be lowered to take the crew ashore.

Some of the crew had to sleep in this dark, airless deck.

When there was not enough cargo, heavy stones were carried in the bottom of the ship. This kept the ship steady. The stones were called ballast.

Food was cooked in the galley. The food was bad and full of beetles called weevils.

## What was it like to be in a battle at sea?

When an enemy ship was sighted, the command was given: "Clear the decks!" Men hurried to clear away hammocks, tables and anything else left lying about. The gunports were opened and the gun crews got ready.

To load a gun, the crew stuffed down the barrel a bag of gunpowder, then a piece of wadding, followed by the cannon ball. The gunpowder was lit through a *touch hole* in the top of the gun.

There was smoke and noise everywhere, and the ship's doctor was kept busy attending to wounded men.

Ships usually sailed into battle with their side to the enemy vessel. Then they could fire *broadsides* at each other. In a broadside, all the guns could be fired together. Galleons usually came quite close to the enemy in a battle.

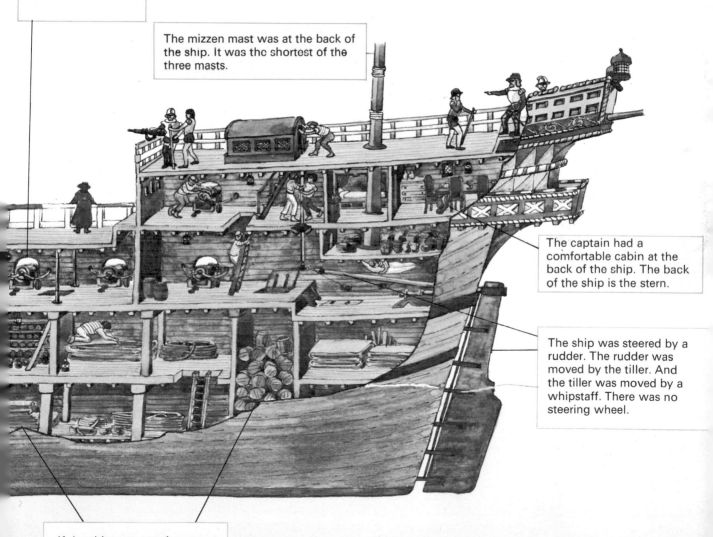

The cannons were fired through holes in the ship's sides called gunports.

The mizzen mast was at the back of the ship. It was the shortest of the three masts.

The captain had a comfortable cabin at the back of the ship. The back of the ship is the stern.

The ship was steered by a rudder. The rudder was moved by the tiller. And the tiller was moved by a whipstaff. There was no steering wheel.

If the ship was carrying cargo it was stored in the holds.

# The Sun King

## Who was the Sun King? Why was he called by that name?

The Sun King was King Louis XIV of France. He lived three hundred years ago, and became one of the most famous kings that France ever had. Louis XIV was called the Sun King because his court was so splendid and grand, his palace so beautiful and Louis such a powerful King, that it seemed as though he glittered like the Sun in the sky. His palace, called Versailles, became as famous as Louis himself.

Above: King Louis and some of his friends sit down for an enormous meal, called a *banquet*. Louis was a big man, and he ate a lot of food at every meal. He liked his friends to eat a lot as well, and got angry if they were not hungry.

## When was the palace of Versailles built for King Louis?

Versailles was begun while Louis was King, but it was not finished until almost a hundred years later. It was the biggest and the grandest palace in the world, and it took a long time to finish decorating all the rooms and the grounds around the palace. The Kings who came after Louis added some extra parts to the palace as well. It all cost so much money, that no one has ever tried to match Versailles.

## What did King Louis do at Versailles?

King Louis and his friends led a very easy life at the Palace. Louis liked to go hunting in the countryside around Versailles, but he also enjoyed walking in the beautiful gardens which had been laid out around the buildings. You can see the King and some of the members of his Court in the gardens, in the picture above. There were hundreds of fountains and statues to look at and admire, and many trees in special tubs.

## Who worked at Versailles?

With so many important people living at the Palace, hundreds of workers were needed there too. Gardeners kept the grounds neat, looked after the flowers and trees, and grew vegetables for food. Everyone had servants to dress them, to keep their rooms clean and tidy, and to cook and serve the food. Grooms cared for the horses and hunting dogs, and kept the coaches ready for journeys. It was a very busy and lively place.

Left: The Palace of Versailles from the front. This picture shows only some of the buildings and the gardens that make up the whole palace.

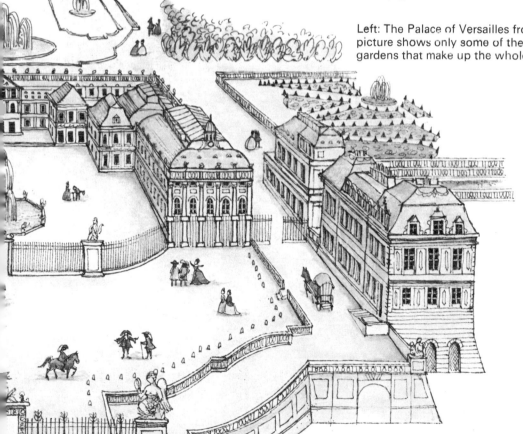

# The American Indians

**Why are the native people of North America called Red Indians?**

The name *Indians* was given to them by an explorer called Columbus. When his ship reached America in 1492, Columbus thought he had found the continent of India! The early settlers in America called the Indians red because their light-brown skin looked red with suntan, to the pale people from the colder lands of Europe.

Apache war-dance

**How did the Indians live?**

Each Indian belonged to a *tribe*, and these were made up of bands of two or three families. All the members of a band looked after each other. They hunted, fished and farmed together, and shared what they had.

There were many different tribes of Indians, who lived in different parts of the country. The Navaho lived in the south-east, and were famous for their beautiful weaving and craft work. The Haida lived in the north-west, by the Pacific Ocean. One of their *totem poles* is shown on the left. Totem poles were carved from wood, and were a record of the tribe's ancestors and gods.

Navaho weaver

Many tribes lived in the central part of America, on the great open plains. Most of these tribes were wanderers, who spent their time following the great herds of buffalo. Their main food was buffalo meat, and they used buffalo skins for clothes, and to make the tents in which they lived. At first, the tribes of the plains hunted buffalo on foot. But after the Spanish settlers brought horses to America, the Indians hunted from horseback. They became excellent riders, and they could shoot a bow and arrow from a galloping horse, without using a saddle or bridle.

Iroquois canoers

Sioux fishermen

## What belongings did the plains Indians own?

When the bands of Indians moved around, all their belongings had to be taken with them. They were all piled up onto wooden frames, and dragged by dogs or horses. The tools, *tepees*, clothes, cooking pots and other materials had to be easy to pack and light to carry. None of the Indian tribes had metal tools. Instead, they used tools made from wood or stone.

## What did the women do?

The women spent a lot of their time preparing the skins of the buffalo their men had killed. The buffalo fur grew thick in winter, and these skins were used for warm mittens, caps and *moccasins* (slippers). Skins from buffalo killed at other times of the year were used for shirts, dresses and the special trousers Indians wore, called *leggings*.

## What did the men do?

Most of the men spent their time hunting buffalo, or other animals they could kill and eat. It was difficult for hunters to spare time for other activities, for it took days to track down, follow and kill enough meat for the whole band.

Below: A group of Indians on the plains of central America. The women are drying skins, and sewing the finished ones into clothes. An Indian baby, wrapped securely in a skin pouch, hangs from the rope of one of the *tepees* – the buffalo skin tents. The chief on the right wears a special head-dress made from feathers, while an Indian in the background sends a signal to another group, using a code of smoke puffs from a fire.

# They Went to a New Land

## Who were the first people who went to live in North America?

The settlers came from many countries, but some of the first were a group of people from England. They were called the Pilgrim Fathers, and they sailed in a small ship called the *Mayflower*. These people settled in a place on the east coast of America, in what is now the state of Virginia.

The Pilgrim Fathers travelled to America because they could not worship as they wished in England. They hoped that in a new land they could lead the sort of life they chose for themselves. They landed in America in 1620.

Below: Two of the Pilgrims in America, with the *Mayflower* in the harbour behind them. The Pilgrims wore plain and simple clothes, to match the sort of worship they wanted for themselves and their families.

## What other people went to America?

There were already people in America, of course. The Indians lived there in tribes, and many of them helped the new arrivals. The Pilgrim Fathers could not have done without Indian help in their first years. But, later, hundreds of thousands of other people left Europe and Asia for the new lands. Many of them were poor, and hoped to find a better start in life there; others went when gold was discovered in California. They hoped to get rich quickly by finding more gold themselves. But life was often dangerous and difficult for the settlers, and it was many years before they lived in safety and comfort.

Potatoes

Tobacco leaf

Tomatoes

Indian corn
(Maize)

Above: Some of the new plants which settlers found in North America.

## How did the settlers live?

The first groups built huts, cleared the land for planting crops, and tried to make a living on the new land. But the plants they brought with them often did not grow well, and they did not understand much about the native ones. Their first years were very hard.

As more and more people arrived in America, they began to annoy the Indian tribes. At first, the Indians had been friendly. But later many of the tribes fought the settlers who wanted their land and food, and who brought guns with them to make their claims.

## Who were the Homesteaders?

As more settlers arrived, many of them travelled west across America in wagons. They wanted the Indians' land for them-selves, and they built homes and fenced off land where they could. A new law said people could claim 160 acres of land in the west, and this was called a *homestead*. Millions of people who had never owned land before saw their chance for a new life. They joined the long journey towards the promised lands in the west.

## What was the journey like?

There were no roads across America then, and no railway went far enough. Most of the settlers travelled in covered wagons, and everything they needed was packed inside, along with the tools and seeds for starting a farm.

Groups of families often travelled to-gether for safety, and to help each other in times of trouble or sickness. The journeys took months.

# The Days of the Cowboys

## Who were the cowboys? Where did they live?

The cowboys were the men who herded the cattle in the west and south of the United States. Cattle had been brought to America by Spanish settlers, and they did well on the *prairie* land. Millions of cattle roamed the country in Texas and other American states. The cattle owners let their animals roam free on the land for most of the year, until it was time for them to be driven to market. Then it was time for the cowboys to do their work. The cattle needed to be rounded up, and taken hundreds – or even a thousand – kilometres to be sold.

Below: A cowboy and his horse, ready for work. Cowboys led a hot, dusty and hard life. But it was a good way for a man who owned nothing to get a start in life in the West. If you could ride, you could get a job as a cowboy.

## What did cowboys wear?

The picture below gives a good idea of the sort of clothes a cowboy needed. The wide-brimmed hat, called a *Stetson*, gave shade from the sun and shelter from rain. The waistcoat and special trousers are made from leather – the trousers are called *chaps*. They guarded the cowboy's legs from cactus and prickly-pear thorns, and lasted well through the long hours he spent on horseback. The cowboy often wore high-heeled boots, too. These helped him keep his feet in the stirrups when he was roping cattle.

The rope on the saddle is called a *lariat*, and was used for cattle. The saddle is broad and comfortable.

## What was branding?

When all the cattle which belonged to different owners roamed together on open land, a way was needed to tell them apart. This was done by branding them with a red-hot iron bar, marked in a special way for each owner. The brand burned a mark on the cattle that stayed forever. You can see some different brand-marks on the right. Branding hurts cattle, but only for a short time. It is still used today because it is a good protection against stealing.

Branding cattle was one of the cowboy's jobs. New calves had to be branded, and all the cattle had to be checked for brands before they could be taken to be sold. The picture below shows cowboys rounding up cattle for branding. The wagon at the side is called a *chuckwagon*. The cowboys took this with them on a round-up. It carried their food supplies.

Star R

Lazy 8

Swinging M

Rocking A

## How long did the cattle drives last?

The cowboys drove the herds of cattle to the nearest market. About 3,000 cattle were taken by 12 cowboys, and they could only travel about 20 or 30 kilometres a day. The cattle travelled slowly so that they would not arrive thin and tired. The drive might take weeks, or even months.

# What Children Wore Long Ago

## Why do children wear different clothes from the kind that adults wear?

Children wear different clothes from adults because they live different kinds of lives. Babies need to wear clothes that will keep them warm, but are easy to move about in. Tight clothes would make it hard for them to wave their arms and legs, or to learn to crawl and walk. Children need the same sort of clothes, so they can run and jump and play. Many adults want their clothes to be different from this. They want to wear clothes that are *fashionable*, even if this means that the clothes are a bit uncomfortable.

But this has not always been so. Years ago, children wore exactly the same sort of clothes as adults wore.

French children in 1066

## Why did children wear adult clothes in the past?

Children used to wear the same clothes as adults, because they were not treated as if they had special needs. People thought that children were just small adults, and the most important thing was to get them ready to be grown-up people. If you look at the pictures on the right, you will see what children wore hundreds of years ago. All these clothes are just the same as the ones that adults wore in those times. None of them are comfortable, and it would be very hard to run or play games while you wore them. The girl's dress from Spain in 1600 had heavy petticoats underneath it, and these made the dress sway when she walked. Children did not have special clothes to wear when they played. They just had to play more carefully than we do today.

A Spanish girl in 1600

## When did all this change?

It is only about two hundred years ago that children began to be thought of as having a life of their own. When that happened, the clothes they were allowed to wear began to change as well. They became looser and more comfortable. Children were encouraged to run and climb, to play ball games, and to have their own kind of fun. Special play clothes were made for them.

English children in 1800

## What did girls wear one hundred years ago?

The girl on the right is getting ready to go out. She is probably going visiting with her mother, and you can see how many different clothes she has to put on. The liberty bodice was lined with stiff bones. It held up the thick cotton stockings with the *suspenders* attached to the bottom edge.

On top of all these things the girl wears a skirt and blouse, and a white apron. On very special occasions she would also wear a petticoat underneath the skirt. Count up the number of different clothes she had to put on, and then count up the clothes you are wearing. How long do you think it took her to get dressed in the morning?

## What did boys wear at the same time?

Boys were a bit luckier than girls, and they did not have to wear quite so many heavy clothes. They wore the same kind of vest and pants, with a thick shirt, short trousers, long socks, and a jacket. Sometimes boys also had to wear a sort of liberty bodice underneath their shirts. The shirts often had high, stiff collars, and boys had to wear a tie around their necks.

## Did all children wear clothes like these?

Not all children did, but these were the clothes that were thought to be best for children. So if your parents did not have enough money to buy you so many clothes, it wasn't a good thing at all! The children were uncomfortable, but at least their friends had to wear the same sorts of things.

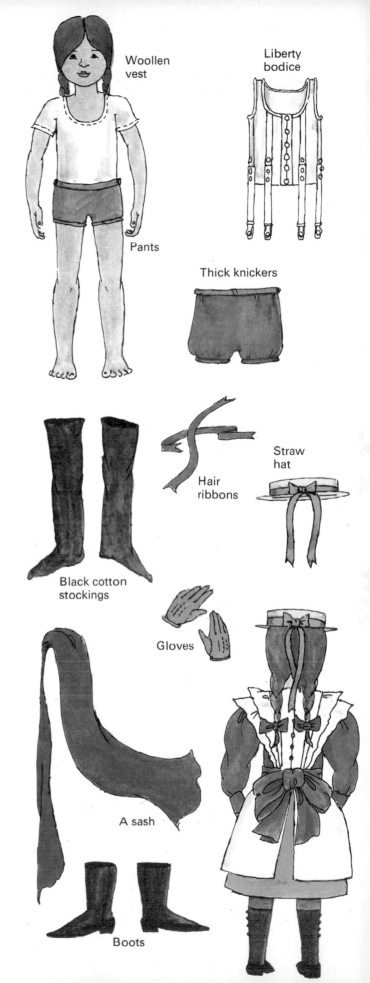

Woollen vest

Liberty bodice

Pants

Thick knickers

Black cotton stockings

Hair ribbons

Straw hat

Gloves

A sash

Boots

# An Old House in Town

Attic

Servant's bedroom

Linen cupboard

Bathroom

Hall

Billiard room

### Who lived in a house like the one on the left?

Only part of the house is shown in the picture. It would have had at least twice as many rooms as the ones you can see. So the family that lived in it would have been quite rich. They would have had at least four or five bedrooms for themselves. The servants' rooms at the top of the house are quite different from the way the family's bedrooms would look. You can see the way in which the billiard room on the ground floor is *decorated*, with wallpaper and thick carpet, paintings and ornaments. Now look at the plain servant's bedroom at the top of the house.

### When was this house built and lived in by the family?

The house was probably built about two hundred years ago, but the picture shows what it looked like only about one hundred years ago. You can tell that from the bathroom on the middle floor. People did not have separate rooms with a bath, water-heater and basin until around 1860.

### How many servants would the family have in their house?

There would be at least five servants in a house like this, and perhaps even more than that. Some of the servants cleaned the house, prepared the rooms and looked after the family's clothes. Other servants did their work in the kitchen, which would have been in the *basement* underground. They cooked all the food, washed the dishes, and did the hard washing and scrubbing work. Servants often worked very long hours each day, and had to get up very early.

### How was the house kept warm in winter?

You can see a coal fire in the billiard room on the ground floor. All the rooms were heated by fires like this one, and they needed to be cleaned out every day, and relit each morning. The coal had to be carried up to the bedrooms as well as the living rooms. Coal fires make a lot of dirt, too, so the rooms had to be dusted and swept all the time. This work was the job of a junior servant, probably the one called an *underhouse parlourmaid*. She had to get up at about 4.00 o'clock in the morning, to do the fires before the family woke up.

### When did people stop living in such big houses?

One hundred years ago, almost everyone who lived in a house could afford to have at least one servant. And without machines to do some of the work, the servants were needed for big houses. But later on, people could no longer afford to pay servants to do so much work for them. They had to live in smaller houses they could look after for themselves.

Bedroom

# Ships of Long Ago

Early people made canoes from fallen logs, and round coracles from animal skins.

The Egyptians found that sails helped their ships to move through the water. They used reeds for ships.

## What were the first ships like?

For thousands of years, the only ships that people made were probably logs. A fallen tree would float in water, and it could be paddled along by hand. Then rough paddles were made from branches, and logs were tied together to make a kind of *raft*. Other kinds of materials, such as reeds, were also used for early ship-building.

Three different types gradually developed. Logs were hollowed out and made into *canoes*. Bundles of reeds were tied together into rafts. And animal skins were used to make round *coracles*.

## How did these ideas grow?

Early boat shapes changed as people found out how they could be made better. And sails were also used, to help the boats move through the water with wind power. The first sail-boats were probably made in Ancient Egypt. It was there, too, that ships were first made from short, narrow planks of wood. This meant that the ships were much safer and faster. The Egyptians sailed all round the Mediterranean with ships like this.

Spanish galleon with three masts.

A fast clipper ship bringing tea from Asia to Europe.

The Greeks built enormous rowing-boats called galleys. They used slaves to row them through the water.

The Vikings were famous ship-builders. Their longboats travelled thousands of miles across the oceans.

## What were the ships used for?

Many countries which developed ships and ship-building used them to make war on other countries. Some ships were used just to explore the land around the seas, lakes and rivers. But the most important use for ships was in trade with other lands. A lot of trade went on in the Mediterranean Sea in ancient times. Wine, oil, honey, metals and spices were all sent by ship among the countries there.

## When did ships get engines?

The first engines were driven by steam. Ships started to have steam engines in the nineteenth century, but sailing ships were still used for another hundred years after that. A fast sailing ship sailed better than the early steam ships, and cost less money to run. Some steamships had paddle-wheels, but then someone thought of the propeller. Propellers worked better, and after a while sailing ships stopped being used.

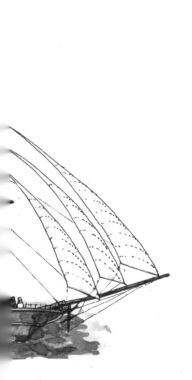

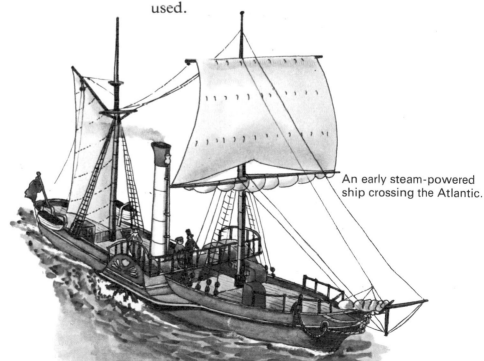

An early steam-powered ship crossing the Atlantic.

# Some Old Trains

This is an old American engine. Its funny-shaped funnel is to stop sparks flying out. These old American trains burned wood instead of coal. There were more sparks from wood. The red thing in front was called a "cow catcher" As the train ran over the great lonely prairies, cattle would often stray on to the line.

The picture on the right shows one of the last steam engines. Now there are very few left. The new engines are cleaner, but they don't look nearly as exciting as the old steam ones.

## When was the Railway Age?

The Railway Age began in 1825. In that year the world's first train carried passengers in the north of England. Crowds came to see the train, and a man on horseback rode in front of it with a red flag. This was to make sure that everyone kept clear.

In the 50 years after this first train ran, almost all our railway system was built. It was then that clever engineers cut all the tunnels, put up all the bridges and laid all the tracks. That was the Railway Age.

## What was it like to travel in one of the first trains?

When the first railways were built, all the passengers travelled in open trucks. They must have become very dirty with smoke from the engine. Soon there came closed carriages for first class passengers.

It was very cold in the first trains. There was no heating in the carriages, but passengers had foot-warmers – usually hot bricks! The bricks were changed when the train stopped somewhere.

# Cars of Yesterday and Today

## When were the first real motor cars made?

From the time that the steam engine was invented, people tried to make cars. But the early steam cars were not very good.

The first real motor cars were sold in Germany by two men called Daimler and Benz. That was in the middle of the 1880s. The car on the right is an early Daimler. It was really a carriage with an engine instead of a horse. But it was driven by a petrol engine, just like the cars of today.

Daimler car of 1886

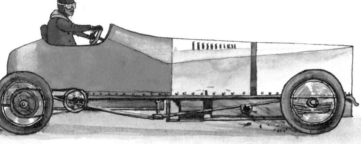

An early racing car

A French Delage of 1913

A "gull-wing" Mercedes 1955

A baby Austin of 1922

## Who first made cars so cheap that they could be bought by many people?

The man who did this was called Henry Ford. In 1908 in the United States he began to make cars quickly and cheaply. These cars were called Model T Fords or the "Tin Lizzie". By 1927 Henry Ford had made 15 million Model Ts.

But the Model T was just the start. In a few years cars became faster, more comfortable and they didn't break down very often.

A double-decker bus of 1912

## How does a car's engine work?

Most cars have petrol engines. If petrol is mixed with air and a spark takes place in the mixture, it explodes. In a car engine there are thousands and thousands of these small explosions happening very quickly. The explosions push cylinders up and down. The cylinders are made to turn the wheels of the car.

The driver can make the car go faster by pressing the *accelerator* pedal with his foot. This makes more petrol go into the engine.

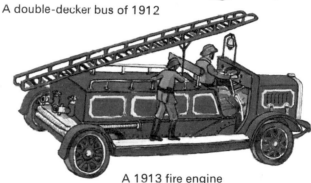

A 1913 fire engine

## Why does a car need a battery?

A car needs a battery for several reasons. It needs a battery to make the sparks that keep the engine working. The battery also works the starter that starts the engine. And it works the lights and the horn.

A coal truck, 1918

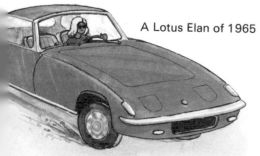

A Lotus Elan of 1965

A petrol tanker of 1923

Powerful cars from many countries take part in motor races.

## For how long have there been car races?

Ever since the car was invented, people have been racing. The first great car race took place in France in 1895. The cars had to race from Paris to Bordeaux and back to Paris, a distance of 1178 kilometres.

There were 13 petrol-driven cars in the race, 6 steam cars and one driven by electricity. The winner was a petrol-driven Panhard. It had wooden wheels with solid rubber tyres and a tiller like a boat's for steering. The car finished the long race at an average speed of 24 kilometres per hour. This was a great feat in those days.

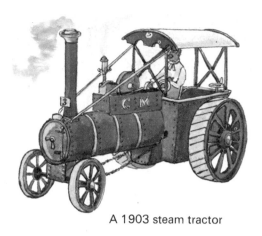
A 1903 steam tractor

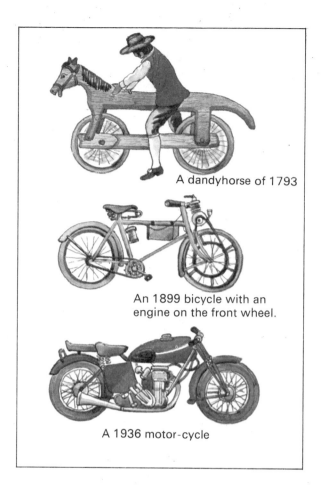
A dandyhorse of 1793

An 1899 bicycle with an engine on the front wheel.

A 1936 motor-cycle

## What other things does a car need?

The car also needs a gearbox. By using the gearbox the driver can use the car's engine as he wants. He *changes gear* for starting off, gaining speed, climbing hills or going fast along a motorway. Some cars have gears that change by themselves. The gears are *automatic*.

And the car's engine needs two other important things. It has to be kept cool. This is usually done by having water in a jacket around the engine. The water is cooled by a fan.

And the engine needs oil. All the hundreds of moving parts in the engine have to be coated with a film of oil so that they run smoothly. If there were no oil the engine would soon grind to a halt.

## How did the motor cycle come about?

The very first bicycles were just pushed along by the rider's feet. They had no pedals and were called "dandyhorses".

The first bicycle with pedals came along in 1865. They were known as "boneshakers" because the seats had no springs.

Bicycles like the ones we know today first appeared in the 1880s. The back wheel was driven by a chain and there were air-filled tyres.

Then someone had the idea of fitting an engine to the bicycle. Actually, the first engines were fitted to three-wheeled tricycles. Daimler, who made one of the first cars, also built one of the first motor-cycles in 1885.

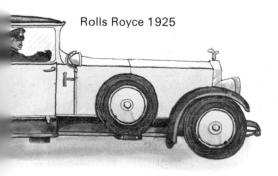
Rolls Royce 1925

Icarus flew too close to the Sun.

# People Began to Fly

A Montgolfier balloon takes off.

### Who was Icarus?

People have always wanted to fly like the birds. There are many, many stories of people flying in ancient myths and legends. One old Greek story tells about a man called Daedalus and his son Icarus. Daedalus and Icarus learned how to fly by attaching birds' feathers to their arms. The feathers were stuck with wax. But Icarus disobeyed his father and flew too close to the Sun. The Sun's heat melted the wax, the feathers came out, and Icarus fell to the ground.

### When did people really learn to fly?

It was not until the year 1783 that a human being really went into the air in a flying machine. The machine was a balloon invented by two brothers called Montgolfier in France. The balloon was just a big bag with a hole at the bottom. The Montgolfiers lit a fire under the hole so that the bag was filled with hot air. Hot air always rises, so the balloon soared high into the air. Then the Montgolfiers attached a basket with a man in it to the bottom of the balloon. Man had learned to fly at last.

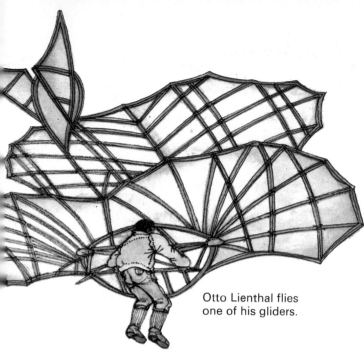

Otto Lienthal flies one of his gliders.

## Why did they build gliders?

In the years after the Montgolfier brothers, people tried all kinds of strange flying machines. Some people thought that the machines should have engines to drive propellers, but no one could make a light enough engine.

So they build gliders and took off from hills, just as hang-gliders do today. One of the most famous of these old glider pilots was Otto Lilianthal, a German. He made more than 2000 glider flights before he was killed.

## Who first flew a proper aeroplane with a propeller?

Two brothers, Orville and Wilbur Wright, had a bicycle shop in Dayton, Ohio, in the United States. When the brothers weren't repairing people's bicycles, they built gliders. With their gliders, the brothers learned all about flying.

Then they built a petrol engine and propellers. They attached these to their latest glider and took their new flying machine to Kitty Hawk in North Carolina. On December 17, 1903, Orville Wright lay down on his face at the controls of *Flyer*, as they called it. As Wilbur ran alongside, *Flyer* bumped along and lifted slowly into the air. That day it flew for only 37 metres, but man had finally taken off in a machine that was heavier than air.

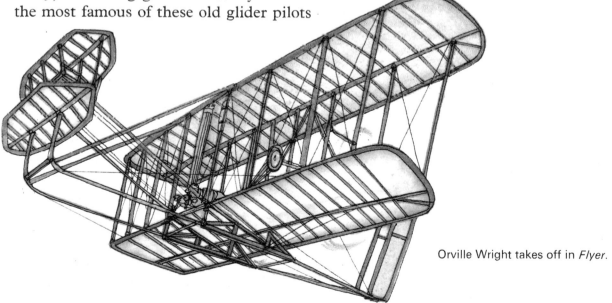

Orville Wright takes off in *Flyer*.

Blériot crossing the Channel.

# Bigger and Better Planes

## Who first flew across the Channel?

In the years after Orville Wright's first flight, people built and flew all kinds of flimsy and strange aeroplanes. In the year 1909 something important happened. Louis Blériot, a famous French airman, took off from Calais in the north of France. Twenty-seven minutes later he landed near Dover castle in the south of England. Blériot had become the first person to fly across the English Channel. For this he won a prize of £1000 offered by the *Daily Mail* newspaper.

## Who first flew across the Atlantic?

The first person to fly across the Atlantic *alone* was a brave American airman called Charles Lindbergh. He did this in 1927 when he flew from New York to Paris. As he touched down in Paris a crowd of 100,000 people was there to greet him.

But an even more daring flight was made by John Alcock and Arthur Whitten Brown. In 1919, eight years before Lindbergh's flight, they flew across the Atlantic from Canada to Ireland in an old World War I bomber. These two were the first to fly across the stormy Atlantic Ocean non-stop.

## What were the first airliners like?

The first airliners to carry passengers were just World War I bombers with extra seats added. Aeroplanes then had no radio and the pilot guided the plane by looking at the ground. The passengers as well as the crew often had to sit in the open.

Then in the 1920s and 1930s airliners grew more comfortable. People sat in special cabins. For long journeys, big flying-boats that could land on water were used.

Up until World War II, all airliners were driven by propellers.

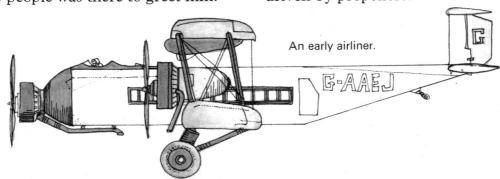

An early airliner.

G-AAEJ

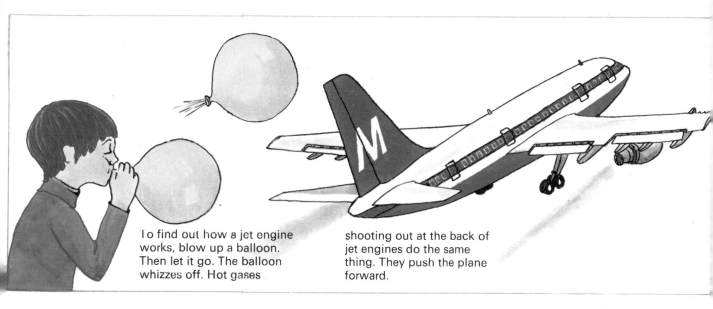

To find out how a jet engine works, blow up a balloon. Then let it go. The balloon whizzes off. Hot gases shooting out at the back of jet engines do the same thing. They push the plane forward.

## What is the difference between a jet engine and one that drives a propeller?

An engine that drives a propeller is really the same as the engine in a motor car. Instead of driving wheels, the engine turns a propeller. A jet engine is quite different. Air is sucked in at the front, mixed with paraffin and squeezed tightly. The mixture of air and paraffin burns fiercely and makes a stream of hot gas that shoots out at the back of the engine. This stream of hot gas pushes the aircraft forward. See the panel about the jet engine at the top of this page.

An early helicopter.

The big jumbo jet below carries 400 people across the Atlantic at a speed of 980 kilometres an hour. It carries enough fuel to let 40 motor cars travel right round the world.

# PLANTS
# AND
# ANIMALS

# What is an Animal?

## What is an animal?

Animals, like plants, are living things. But unlike plants, most animals cannot make their own food. They must find their food around them, and so most animals can move. There are animals that crawl, run, hop, climb or fly.

Over a million different kinds of animal live on Earth. They range from tiny creatures too small to see to the blue whale, at 29 metres the biggest animal on Earth.

## How do animals breathe?

Almost all animals need the oxygen in air to stay alive. Some, such as insects and earthworms, take in oxygen through their skins. Fish breathe through gills, which can take

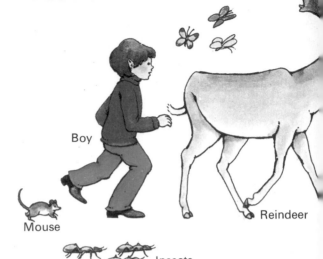

Butterflies

Boy

Mouse

Reindeer

Insects

Animals move in different ways. Some crawl, others hop, fly slither, walk or run. Most mammals walk on all fours. Only a few, including humans, can walk upright on their hind legs. All insects have six legs, and crawl or fly.

### How are animals born?

Birds and most reptiles lay eggs. The young animals grow by feeding on food inside the egg until they are ready to hatch out.

Bird's nest

Turtle eggs

A mammal gives birth to live young. The young mammal grows inside its mother's body until it is ready to be born. It drinks milk from its mother's body until it is old enough to find its own food. Many mammals are ready to look after themselves after only a few days, weeks or months. Others, such as young elephants or tigers, stay with their mothers for more than a year. Human children stay the longest with their parents – often more than 15 years.

Zebras

Bird

Yak

Horse

Cat

oxygen out of the water. Mammals, from dolphins to people, have lungs. They breathe in oxygen and breathe out carbon dioxide gas.

## What do animals eat?

Animals find their food in different ways. Insects eat plants, or other insects. Spiders trap their prey in webs. Meat-eating animals, called carnivores, have sharp teeth and claws.

Animals grow to be roughly the same size as their parents. The giraffe starts out life at about $1\frac{1}{2}$ metres high and weighing 70 kilograms. By the time it is grown up, it may reach over 5 metres and weigh 900 kilograms.

# The World of Dinosaurs

## What sort of animals were the dinosaurs?

The dinosaurs were reptiles – and like reptiles today, they had tough scaly skins. They laid eggs on land, from which their babies hatched. But they were not like today's reptiles in any other way. Some were as tall as a four-storey building, and as heavy as twenty elephants. Some ate only plants, but others were meat-eaters. The dinosaurs lasted for millions of years.

## Which dinosaurs were the biggest?

The biggest ones were the plant-eating dinosaurs, like the *Diplodocus* below. It used its tail to defend itself. A plant-eating dinosaur called *Brachiosaurus* was also enormously big.

*Stegosaurus* had a spiky back.

*Orthinomimus* was a small dinosaur.

*Tyrannosaurus* was a meat-eating dinosaur.

# What was special about dinosaurs?

The dinosaurs were different from the reptiles that came before them in some important ways. Early reptiles rested their bellies on the ground. They could move only by wriggling their bodies from side to side. But the dinosaurs legs were underneath their bodies, like most mammals' legs are today. This meant that dinosaurs could move their legs backwards and forwards, rather than having to use their legs as oars. They could stand, walk and run more easily, and they could move much faster than any other reptiles.

Some people now think that dinosaurs were warm-blooded animals. If that is true, they would have moved very fast indeed. They could have galloped around the land after their food.

Above: *Pteranodon* was a reptile that learned to use the air instead of the ground for its home. It probably did not really fly, but instead glided around on currents of wind. You can see from the picture that *Pteranodon* still had its front "arms" attached to its wings. The scaly claws are still there, but they would not have been much use.

Below: During the time of the dinosaurs, many new plants began to grow. The first mammals lived at the same time as the first dinosaurs, but they were very small creatures. They hid away from the dangerous meat-eating reptiles.

*Diplodocus* was a plant-eating dinosaur.

# More Dinosaurs

Above: A plant-eating dinosaur called a *Triceratops*. It had armour and horns to defend itself against its enemies.

**Where did dinosaurs live?**

Many dinosaurs lived on land, but some learned to live in the air. These dinosaurs were the ancestors of the first birds in the world.

There were dinosaurs in the seas as well. Life had first begun in the water, and some reptiles learned to live there. Many of them developed rows of sharp teeth and ate fish, while others probably used worms, water snails and plants for their food.

The dinosaur in the picture below is called a *Plesiosaur*. It lived in the sea and hunted fish for its food. It had flippers rather than fins, and used its tail like a rudder.

Some people believe that the Loch Ness monster, if it really exists, may be descended from a Plesiosaur. If that is true, it is the only dinosaur that still lives. Dinosaurs died out millions of years ago.

**Why did dinosaurs die out?**

The dinosaurs lived longer on Earth than people have done so far, so they were very successful creatures. No one knows for sure why they died out, but there are some suggestions to think about. It may be that the new plants which developed in those times were not good for them to eat. It might be that the Earth became too cold for such large reptiles to survive. Some people think that changes in the weather were not

*Plesiosaurs* lived in the sea and hunted fishes for food.

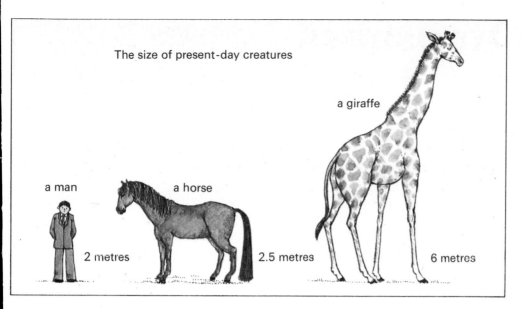

The size of present-day creatures

a giraffe

a man

a horse

2 metres

2.5 metres

6 metres

Left: Some dinosaurs were much bigger than even the tallest animals today. A *Brachiosaurus* could be as tall as 12.6 metres – more than twice as tall as the giraffe! But some dinosaurs were as small as chickens.

just colder ones, but hotter ones as well. Perhaps the dinosaur's bodies could not cope with sudden heat-waves or snow-storms!

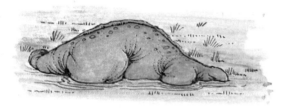

## How do we know what dinosaurs looked like?

We know what dinosaurs looked like from the *fossils* which have been found. This

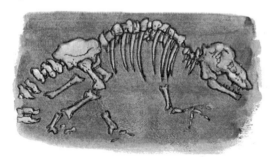

picture shows a dinosaur dying in some mud. The mud covers it up, and soon only the skeleton is left. After a long time, the bones turn into fossils in the dry mud. The mud becomes rock. If the rock moves, the fossil may be brought up to the surface of

the ground. Scientists may find it there, and chip the rock away.

Next, scientists try to put the fossil bones back together again. All the pieces are cleaned and studied. They are compared with the bones of modern animals. This helps scientists work out just which bones belong together. Others fossils can help as well. If some bones are missing, another fossil might show what they would look

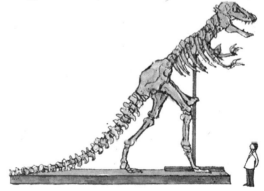

like. The scientists also find out how old the fossil is.

Now the fossil pieces can be put together properly. This is the model made from the dead dinosaur. It shows how the dinosaur – a *Tyrannosaurus* – looked inside. It shows how it could have moved and lived. But it does not show what colour the dinosaur was. No one knows that.

# Animals of Cold Lands

### What do seals eat?

Many kinds of seals live in the cold waters around the north and south poles. Most of them feed on fish. The Bearded seal eats crabs and shellfish, but the shells from these creatures have never been found in the seals' stomachs. Scientists think the seals must be able to break open the shells and eat the insides. The Leopard seal eats penguins. The Crab-eater seal does not eat crabs. It prefers to eat tiny shrimp-like animals called *krill*, which it sieves from the water with its teeth.

Above: The hooded seal can puff up loose skin on its head to make a cushion-like hood.

Below: The elephant seal gets its name from the male's big, lumpy nose, which looks a bit like an elephant's trunk.

### Do animals have winter coats?

In cold lands, some animals change their fur or feathers to match the winter snow. The brown stoat becomes white with a dark tip to its tail. The Arctic fox and the ptarmigan also put on winter colours. They are hard to see against the snow, so are safer from enemies. They can also hunt without being seen.

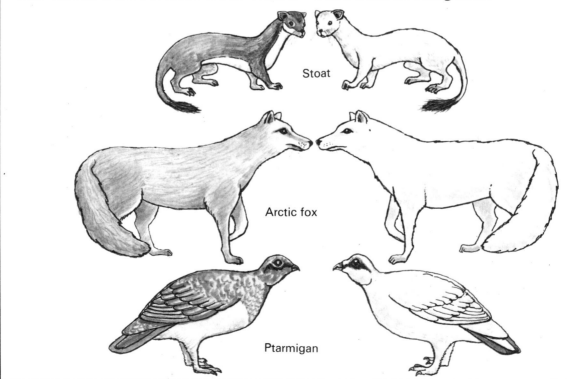

Stoat

Arctic fox

Ptarmigan

78

The polar bear hunts fish and seals. Unlike other bears, it eats only meat.

The caribou travels hundreds of miles south in the autumn to escape the arctic winter.

The snowy owl eats small animals.

The musk ox's long, shaggy coat keeps it warm.

The Brent goose flies south in the winter.

## How long can seals stay under water?

Like land mammals, seals breathe air into their lungs. But they can swim and fish under water for much longer than most other mammals, including man. Scientists have studied Weddell seals in the Antarctic. These seals will dive to 300 or 400 metres. They usually stay under water for about 20 minutes, but sometimes stay down for as long as 40 minutes.

## Where do reindeer live?

Reindeer are a kind of deer that lives in cold arctic lands. There are reindeer in northern Scandinavia and Russia. The Lapps of Scandinavia keep herds of reindeer. The reindeer give the Lapps food and clothing They pull sledges.

The reindeer of North America are called *caribou*. This is the American Indian word for reindeer. Most caribou live in Canada and Greenland.

Polar bears dig dens in the snow for their cubs. Two cubs are born in January. They are no bigger than guinea pigs.

The cubs stay with their mother in the den until early summer.

Polar bears sometimes swim under water. Mostly they do a "dog paddle" with their heads above water.

# About Penguins

Emperor penguin

Macaroni penguin

King penguin

Peruvian penguin

## Where do penguins live?

All penguins live south of the Equator. Many live around the icy shores of Antarctica. Some penguins live along the southern tips of Africa and South America, and in southern New Zealand and Australia. There are even penguins as far north as the Galapagos Islands, off northern South America. But there are no penguins in the Arctic.

## Can penguins fly?

Penguins cannot fly. They are built for life in the water. Their wings are more like flippers, and are used for swimming. On land, penguins wadfle or hop. They are clumsy but funny to watch. In the water, they are fast and graceful swimmers. Penguins have thick layers of fat and feathers on their bodies to keep them warm. In the summer, when temperatures climb to above freezing, penguins keep "cool" by holding their flippers away from their bodies.

## How do penguins play?

Penguins live together in large groups, or colonies. On land, they often seem to be having fun. Sometimes they march in lines like soldiers. Often they slide down icy slopes on their stomachs. They chase each other, or jump in and out of the water. Unlike most birds, penguins are not afraid of people. They are curious and will walk straight up to visitors to their colonies. They can be caught very easily.

## Do penguins build nests?

Most penguins build nests on the ground out of pebbles, grass or sticks. Some nest in burrows. The Emperor and King penguins do not make nests. They lay just one egg on floating sea ice. The male Emperor penguin keeps the egg warm on his feet for over 60 days. He covers it with a fold of skin. During this time he has nothing to eat. When the young penguin hatches, the female returns to look after it, and the male goes off to find food.

Half-grown penguin chicks are collected in groups called crèches. They are covered with thick, fluffy feathers and they huddle together to keep warm. Even though they all look exactly alike, each parent penguin can find its own chick in the group.

Adélie penguins build nests of small stones. When it is mating time, the male Adélie penguin offers the female a stone. If she accepts, he knows she will be his mate. Together, the two penguins build the nest. Adélie penguins sometimes make their nests miles from the sea. They must walk for days to find food.

Penguins swim well and are at home in the sea. On land they can be funny to watch.

Sometimes penguins slide.

Penguins cannot fly. Their wings are more like flippers.

They walk and run.

They swim.

They jump out of the water.

They jump into the water.

They dive and use their flippers to push themselves along.

# The Busy Beaver

### Where do beavers live?

Beavers build their homes in lakes and rivers, but they search for their food on the dry land around the water. So, although they need water, they also need the bark of trees for food, and the branches and twigs from which to build their homes.

Although beavers are excellent swimmers, they cannot breathe under water. Their homes, called *lodges*, are built above the water's level. The entrances to the lodges, however, are underneath the water. This helps the beaver to protect itself against its enemies.

If a beaver is threatened by an enemy such as a wolf, it immediately makes for the water. Before it dives it will slap the water with its broad tail. The noise this makes will warn other beavers that danger is about. Then the beaver dives under the water, perhaps to swim to its lodge. It can stay under the water for up to 15 minutes, without having to come up for air.

Above: the beaver's dense fur acts like a wet suit and keeps its skin dry. Its ears and nose close up when it is under the water, and its tail makes a very good rudder.

## What sort of animal is the beaver?
## What makes it different from others?

Beavers are rodents, like rats and mice. Like other rodents they have front paws which are shaped to hold food, and long front teeth for gnawing. But beavers have very unusual back feet, and a tail that is just right for a beaver's way of life.

The back feet are webbed, like a duck's. This helps the beaver to swim fast and well through the water. Beavers' tails are useful as rudders for swimming, but they make excellent supports when the beavers are cutting trees. Using its tail, a beaver can balance neatly on a branch, or prop itself up comfortably, while it sits on the ground beside a tree.

The beaver's hind feet are webbed for swimming.

## Why do beavers cut down trees?

Beavers need to have level water around their lodges, or these may flood. Sometimes they build dams, to make sure the river or lake does not disturb their homes.

These dams are built from trees, which the beavers cut down with their sharp front teeth. They are very skilled at this work – one beaver can gnaw through a medium-sized tree in about 20 minutes! Then the branches are dragged to the water, floated into position by the swimming beavers, and woven into a firm, sturdy structure.

Beavers also use logs and branches to build their lodges. The inside is lined with smaller twigs, mixed with mud. It is warm and dry, and very snug in the winter.

At one time, beavers were common all over Europe and in northern Asia. Now they are found only in north America and in Sweden.

# Animals of the African Plains

### What is a "troop" of baboons?

Baboons live together in groups called troops. Most baboon troops have from 20 to 80 baboons in them, but some have as many as 150. The baboons in a troop follow certain rules. Often the strongest male is troop leader, though sometimes there are several leaders. The younger, weaker males and all the females must obey the leaders. The leaders protect the females, especially those with babies.

All the baboons in one troop move around the plains together. Sometimes the troop will settle near a herd of antelope. The antelope are alert and warn the baboons of danger. In return, the baboons often frighten off leopards or cheetahs.

### Why does a zebra have stripes?

Close up, a zebra's stripes are bold and easy to see. But at a distance, the zebra's stripes actually help to hide it, even on the open plains. A herd of zebra seen from far away is

Zebra

Elephant

Waterbuck

Wart hogs

Hyena

Lion

Leopard

Vulture

Wild dog

Above: Some mammals of the African plains. The lion and the leopard are both members of the cat family. Hyenas and wild dogs are scavengers.

Baboons

Lions

Snake    Marabou stork

much more difficult to see than, say, a herd of wildebeest, which are all one colour. Stripes also help zebras to recognize one another. Each zebra has its own stripe pattern much as we have our very own fingerprints.

## Who are the scavengers of the plains?

Animal scavengers are those that do not usually hunt for their own food. They eat animals that have died or been killed. Hyenas and wild dogs often move in to eat the "leftovers" from a lion's kill. Sometimes, if only one or two lions are feeding, a pack of hyenas will chase the lions away and take over the carcass. If they are hungry enough, hyenas and wild dogs will hunt in packs for their own food. They tire out their prey by chasing it for miles until it drops.

Some birds are scavengers too. Vultures are quick to spot dead animals from the air. The marabou stork also feeds on animal leftovers.

## How do plains animals "share" food?

Many of the animals of the African plains are *herbivores* – that is, they eat only plants. The plains are covered with dry grass, low scrubby bushes and a few trees. If all the herbivores ate the same plants, there would not be enough food to go round. But we now know that they eat very different foods. Antelopes eat the fine, softer grasses.

Zebras eat tougher grasses. Rhinoceroses feed on low shrubs. Elephants and giraffes can reach the leaves on trees. Even they "share" their food. The elephants eat leaves from the lowest branches. Giraffes, which are taller, feed on leaves higher up.

Giraffe

Elephant

Black rhino

Weaver birds

Ostrich

African buffalo

Below: The tropical grasslands of Africa are known as the savanna. Many large animals live on the savanna, including the largest of all land animals – the elephant. Giraffes roam where there are trees. But the most common animals of the plains are the great herds of antelope, including the eland, impala and wildebeest. The ostrich, the world's largest bird, also makes its home on the plains.

## Which birds "weave" their nests?

The weaver birds of Africa are small birds related to the house sparrows of Europe. They weave complicated hanging nests from grass and leaves. Often the nests are rounded with a tube-like entrance One tree may have 50 or 60 nests hanging from it. The male weaver builds the nest.

## Which is the fastest animal on land?

The African plain is home for the world's fastest land animal – the cheetah. Cheetahs have been timed at speeds up to 114 kilometres an hour over short distances. A cheetah must catch its prey quickly, for it cannot keep up its fast speed for long.

Giraffe

Eland

Impala

Cheetah

Vervet monkey

## Why is the giraffe at home on the plains?

Giraffes are specially built for life on the plains. They use their long legs to run fast. Their long necks can stretch up to reach leaves in the trees where most other animals cannot browse. During the dry season, giraffes can go for many days without water. They get the water they need from the leaves they eat. When they do find water, giraffes spread their front legs wide to lower their heads to drink. Despite the length of its neck a giraffe has the same number of neck bones as we do, though each bone is 40 cm long.

# In the Jungle

### How big is a python's dinner?

Pythons are large snakes that live in Africa and Asia. Some kinds grow to over 9 metres long. Pythons mostly feed on small mammals, but the larger African pythons sometimes kill small antelopes weighing up to 54 kilograms. All pythons squeeze their prey to death.

### Which jungle animal is related to the giraffe?

Deep in the African rain forest lives a shy, quiet creature called an okapi. It looks a bit like a small horse. Despite its size, it was not discovered by zoologists until 1901. Like a giraffe, an okapi has small horns partly covered with skin, but it does not have a long neck.

### Why do hippos "yawn"?

Hippos spend most of their time in the water, lying partly submerged. Sometimes they open their mouths wide, as though they are yawning. But this is really a sign to other hippos that they are angry. Male hippos often fight, giving each other nasty wounds with their teeth.

Grey parrots

Blue flycatcher

Green mamba

Tree frog

Mandrill

Spoonbill

Shoebill stork

Hippopotamus

Potto

Python

Diana monkey

Turaco

Leopard

Chimpanzee

Chameleon

Gorilla

Okapi

# Some Strange Animals

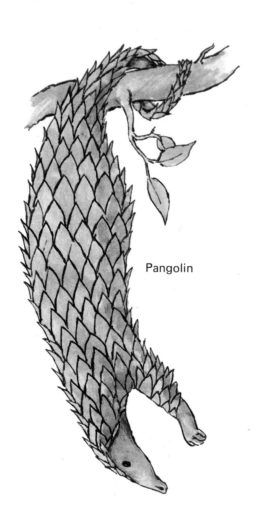

Three-toed sloth

### Why do sloths hang upside-down?

Sloths have long hooked claws on each of their feet. These are used when they climb around the trees in tropical America, where they live. Sloths are quite heavy for climbing animals, and can weigh up to 4 kg, but the upside-down movement is a good one for them. Their claws, long arms and legs, and curling tail make sure that they are secure on the branches. It is much safer for the sloths to climb and hang like this, than to risk slipping off the branch the other way up! Upside-down life means that sloths do not have to worry about *balance*.

### Why do pangolins curl into a ball?

Pangolins hang upside-down from trees by their tails, but they also curl into a tight ball if danger threatens. The hard scales which cover their bodies help to protect them. If a mother pangolin has her baby with her, she will wrap herself around her baby as well. Her scales will protect both of them.

Pangolins are ant-eating animals, and they live in Africa and in the tropical parts of Asia.

Pangolin

A pangolin curled up

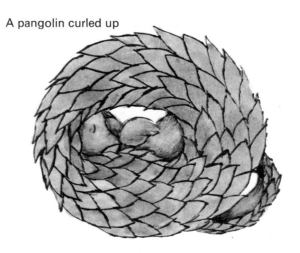

## Why do skunks make a dreadful smell?

Skunks make a smell to protect themselves from their enemies – and the smell is such a bad one that this works very well!

The skunk's distinctive colouring warns other animals to keep away, and most do. But sometimes a careless dog will try to attack a skunk. The skunk then raises its tail and sends out a squirt of liquid from a special *gland*. The liquid can travel for over 2 metres, and it sticks to whatever it touches. The smell lasts for days, and only skunks find it pleasant.

Skunks have such an excellent defence that they are seldom worried about danger. Only owls are any real threat to them. These birds can swoop down from above and seize a small skunk before it can use its smell.

Skunk

## Which birds lay their eggs in deep holes?

The puffin is a strange-looking seabird. During the breeding season, the male puffin's big beak becomes brightly coloured. The female bird lays a single egg in a hole. This hole may be a metre deep.

## Which animals can grow a new tail?

There are thousands of different kinds of lizards. Most of them look like snakes with legs because they have very long tails. Some lizards have a strange way of protecting themselves. If an enemy bites the lizard's tail, the lizard just scampers off, leaving its tail behind. And the tail keeps wriggling for quite a while. After a while, the lizard grows a new tail.

The strange puffin

The lizard's tail

# Strange Animals from Australia

## Why do kangaroos have pouches?

Kangaroos belong to a group of mammals called *marsupials*. A young marsupial, like the young of most other mammals, is born alive. But it is born very early compared to other young mammals. It is tiny and has no fur. It cannot see. As soon as it is born, it climbs up its mother's fur and into her pouch. There, it attaches itself to a teat from which it drinks milk.

The tree kangaroo spends its life in the trees. It cannot jump like other kangaroos. Its feet have long, curved claws to help it cling to the branches as it feeds.

Right: A young kangaroo gets a free ride in its mother's pouch. A young kangaroo is called a joey.

The koala is another marsupial from Australia. When the young koala is big enough to leave its mother's pouch, it clings to the fur on her back as she climbs through the trees.

A baby kangaroo grows inside its mother's pouch for about five months before it even pokes its head out to look round. It will begin to leave the pouch for a little while when it is about six months old. When this baby leaves the pouch for good, a new baby kangaroo is born almost immediately and crawls up to take its place in the pouch.

## The platypus swims like a fish, lays eggs like a duck and has fur like a mammal. Which is it?

The platypus is one of the very few mammals that lay eggs. It lives along the banks of rivers and streams in Australia and Tasmania. It has a wide bill like a duck which it uses to find shellfish and insects in the soft mud at the bottom of rivers.

The platypus lays two or three eggs in a burrow lined with grass and leaves. When the young platypuses hatch out, they climb onto their mother and lick milk that oozes from under the fur on her stomach. They come out of the burrow for the first time when they are a few months old. They growl, squeak and play like puppies.

## Which bird decorates its house?

The male bowerbird of Australia and New Guinea has a special way of attracting a mate. He builds a kind of shelter, or bower, out of sticks. Sometimes the bower has two walls and a floor. Other bowers are inside a tunnel of sticks. The bowerbird collects brightly coloured shells, flowers, leaves and dead insects to decorate his bower. Then he dances and whistles to attract the female inside. They mate inside the bower. Afterwards, the female leaves to build a nest for her eggs.

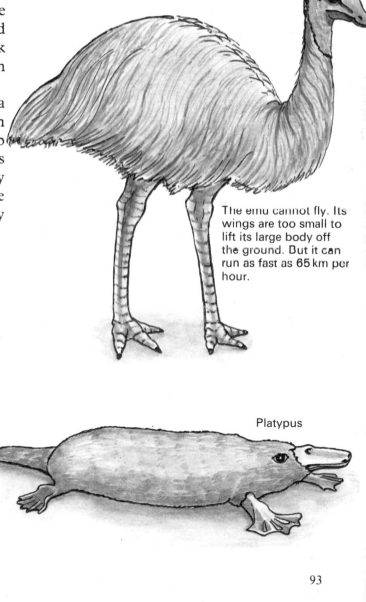

The emu cannot fly. Its wings are too small to lift its large body off the ground. But it can run as fast as 65 km per hour.

Bowerbird

Platypus

# Looking at Reptiles

### Why don't reptiles have fur?

Snakes, tortoises, turtles, alligators, crocodiles and lizards are all reptiles. They have scaly skins. Tortoises' and turtles' bodies are inside a bony shell. But no reptile has fur. This is because reptiles' bodies are the same temperature as the air around them. Mammals, which have fur, are different. Their bodies stay at one temperature all the time. Their fur keeps this temperature steady even in cold weather. Reptiles must keep their temperature steady by moving around. A desert lizard sits in the sun in the morning, as the sun warms the earth. When it gets too hot, the lizard moves under a rock for shade. At night when it is cool, the lizard stays warm in its burrow under the ground.

### When is a tortoise at home?

Tortoises and turtles are always at home. They carry their homes around on their backs. These homes are heavy, bony shells. A tortoise is clumsy and moves slowly. It cannot run away from attackers. When it is frightened, it can pull its head and legs into its shell for protection.

Most tortoises live in warm places. Giant tortoises nearly two metres long live on the Galapagos Islands in the Pacific.

Above: The alligator is built for life in the water. It swims by moving its long tail from side to side.

Right: A tortoise tucks itself under its shell for safety. It will sleep, or *hibernate*, during the winter.

Below: Many people like to keep tortoises as pets. They do not have teeth, but can tear food into small pieces with the hard edges of their jaws. Pet tortoises like lettuce and other leafy vegetables to eat.

## Is it an alligator or a crocodile?

Alligators and crocodiles look very much alike. They are both built for swimming, with long, cigar-shaped bodies. They have long snouts and strong jaws with rows of sharp teeth. Their backs are covered with bony plates and scales. They eat fish, birds and small mammals. Like other reptiles, they lay leathery eggs. There is only one easy way to tell an alligator from a crocodile. The teeth in an alligator's lower jaw fit into little pockets in its upper jaw when the alligator shuts its mouth, so only the upper teeth can be seen. When a crocodile shuts its mouth, you can still see all its teeth. One larger tooth at the side actually sticks up above its upper "lip".

The frilled lizard lives in Australia. When it is in danger, it raises its frill in a wide circle round its head to make itself look big and frightening to enemies.

## What can snakes do that we can't?

Most snakes lay eggs. A few give birth to live young.

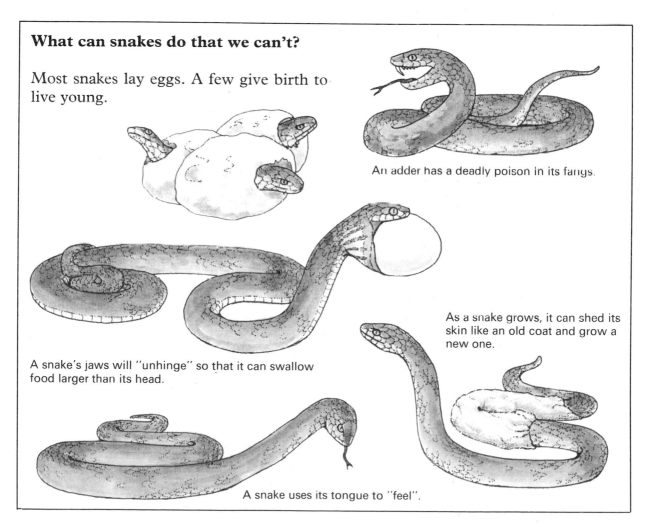

An adder has a deadly poison in its fangs.

A snake's jaws will "unhinge" so that it can swallow food larger than its head.

As a snake grows, it can shed its skin like an old coat and grow a new one.

A snake uses its tongue to "feel".

# Is it an Insect?

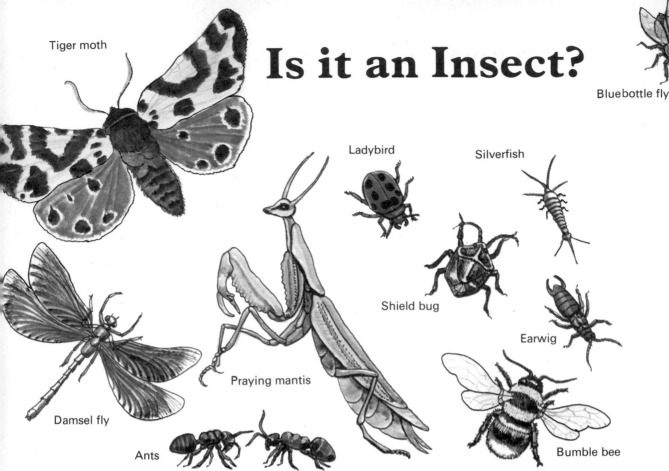

Tiger moth

Bluebottle fly

Damsel fly

Praying mantis

Ants

Ladybird

Silverfish

Shield bug

Earwig

Bumble bee

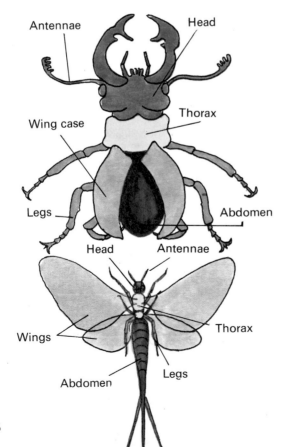

Antennae

Head

Wing case

Thorax

Legs

Abdomen

Head

Antennae

Wings

Thorax

Abdomen

Legs

## What is an insect?

All the animals on this page are insects. There are millions of different kinds of insects – butterflies and moths, beetles, bees, ants, flies and grasshoppers.

Insects do not have backbones. Their bodies are divided into three parts: the head, the *thorax* and the *abdomen*. The head has a pair of feelers, or *antennae*. Insects have 6 legs.

Insects live everywhere except in the sea. Some live in pools of boiling hot water that spouts up from the earth. Others live in the always-frozen polar regions. They can feed on almost anything – plants, animals, even plastic.

Many insects are pests. They damage crops and spread disease. Some harmful insects are mosquitos, locusts, flies and fleas. But some insects are useful. They take pollen from one flower to another, and do other useful jobs.

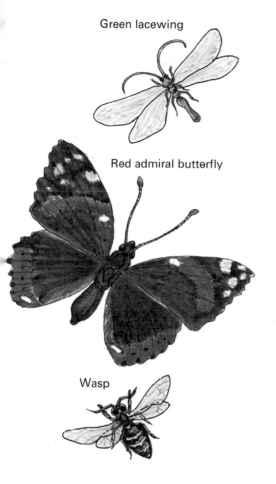

Green lacewing

Red admiral butterfly

Wasp

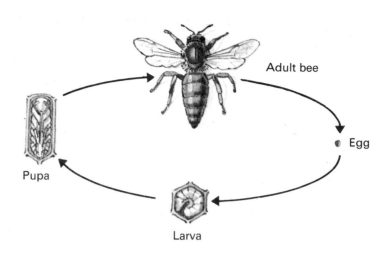

Adult bee

Egg

Pupa

Larva

## How do most insects grow?

Many insects go through four stages in their lives. At each stage they are different. The insect is born as an egg. The egg hatches into a grub, or *larva*. After a while the larva turns into a *pupa* or *chrysalis*. The adult insect grows inside the pupa and breaks out when it is fully formed.

## How big are insects?

Insects are all different sizes. Some are so small that you can hardly see them – smaller than the full-stops on this page. Others are big. The heaviest is the Goliath beetle which lives in Africa. It can weigh as much as 100 grams and be 120 millimetres long. There is a stick insect that also lives in hot countries and is 330 millimetres long. It looks just like a long twig. And there is a huge moth called the Atlas moth whose wings would cover this page.

## How long do insects live?

Insects do not live long. Most live for only a few weeks. And some, like mayflies, live only a few hours. But a queen bee may live for 7 years.

## Are these insects?

Look at the creatures in the picture below. Which of them do you think are insects? The answer is that none of them are. None of them has 6 legs.

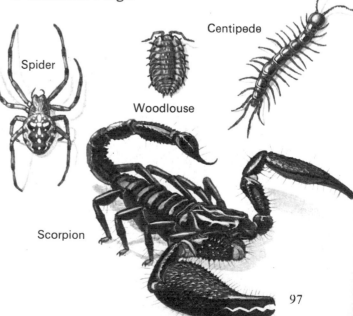

Spider

Woodlouse

Centipede

Scorpion

97

# The Busy Bees

Pollen basket

## Are all bees the same?

No. There are many different kinds of bees, but the best known kind is the honey bee. Bumblebees live in smaller nests than honey bees, and they make very little honey. The picture below shows a bumblebee.

There are three different kinds of honey bee – *queens, workers* and *drones*. They all have different jobs to do.

## What do the different bees do?

Honey bees live in *hives*. Each hive or colony has about 50,000 worker bees. Worker bees are female, but they do not breed. Each colony has a queen bee which breeds. It also has a few hundred drones, which are male bees. Drones do not have a sting.

The worker bee's life is very short. It only lives for about four weeks, so the queen bee has to keep laying eggs very quickly. She does this to make sure that there are enough bees. From time to time a new queen is born. The old queen then leaves the hive with about half the workers to seek another home.

Some people keep bees for their honey in wooden hives. The worker bees make honeycomb on special frames in the hive. The beekeeper in the picture below is using smoke to calm the bees while he takes the honey from the hive.

## What goes on inside the hive?

Inside the hive of the honey bee are cells made of wax. The queen lays her eggs in the cells. Larvae hatch out of the eggs and are fed by the worker bees. The larvae then become pupas before they come out as adult bees.

Worker bees collect nectar and pollen from flowers. The nectar is made into honey. It is stored in the hive to feed the bees. The workers also build the new nest from wax which they make inside their bodies. They chew the wax and make the six-sided cells of the honeycomb with it.

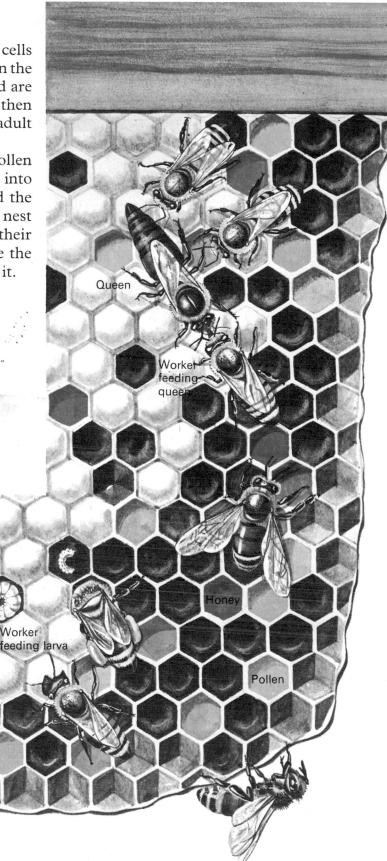

Hive

INSIDE THE HIVE

Queen

Worker feeding queen

Pupa

Worker feeding larva

Honey

Pollen

# Butterflies and Moths

## What is the difference between a butterfly and a moth?

Butterflies and moths are very much alike. But there are some differences between them. Butterflies usually flutter about during the day. Most moths come out at night and rest during the day.

Butterflies rest with their wings folded upwards. Moths rest with their wings spread out flat. Butterflies have little knobs at the ends of their feelers (the feelers are called *antennae*). Most moths have hair-like or feathery antennae.

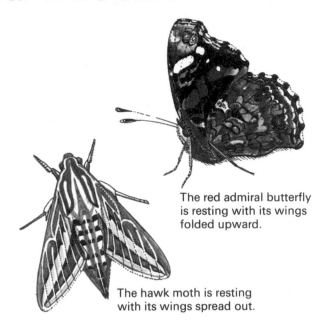

The red admiral butterfly is resting with its wings folded upward.

The hawk moth is resting with its wings spread out.

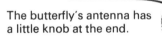

The butterfly's antenna has a little knob at the end.

The moth's antenna is feathery.

## What do butterflies and moths feed on?

Most butterflies and moths feed on a sweet liquid called *nectar*. They suck up the nectar from flowers through a long tube-like tongue called a *proboscis*. They find the flowers by smelling them with their antennae.

This peacock butterfly has uncurled a long tube called a proboscis. It uses this tube to suck up nectar from the flowers.

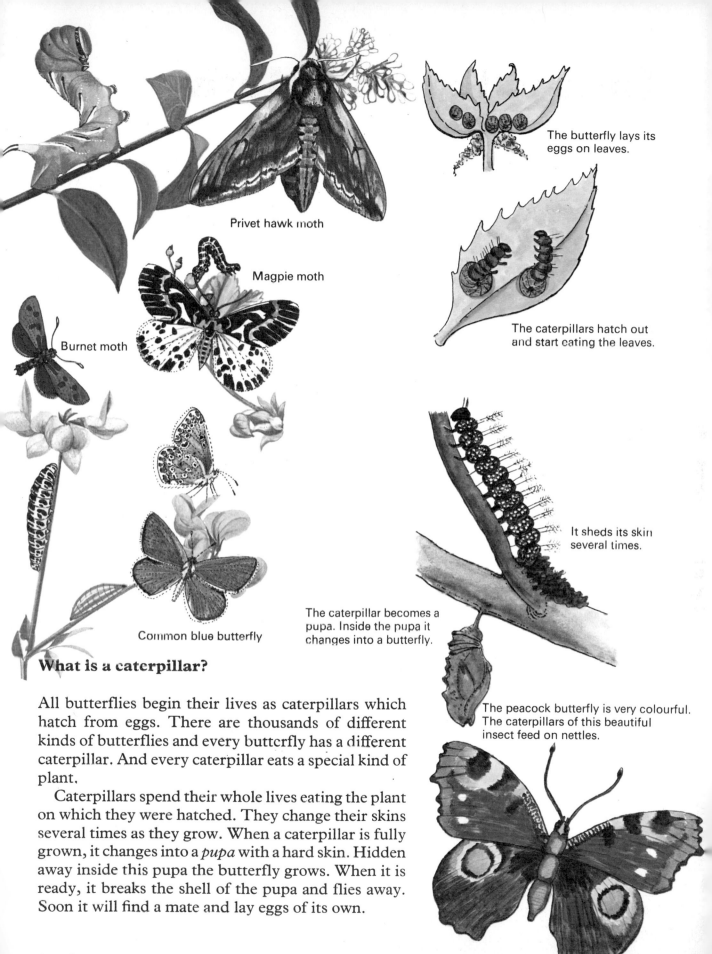

Privet hawk moth

Magpie moth

Burnet moth

Common blue butterfly

The butterfly lays its eggs on leaves.

The caterpillars hatch out and start eating the leaves.

It sheds its skin several times.

The caterpillar becomes a pupa. Inside the pupa it changes into a butterfly.

The peacock butterfly is very colourful. The caterpillars of this beautiful insect feed on nettles.

## What is a caterpillar?

All butterflies begin their lives as caterpillars which hatch from eggs. There are thousands of different kinds of butterflies and every butterfly has a different caterpillar. And every caterpillar eats a special kind of plant.

Caterpillars spend their whole lives eating the plant on which they were hatched. They change their skins several times as they grow. When a caterpillar is fully grown, it changes into a *pupa* with a hard skin. Hidden away inside this pupa the butterfly grows. When it is ready, it breaks the shell of the pupa and flies away. Soon it will find a mate and lay eggs of its own.

# The Ant World

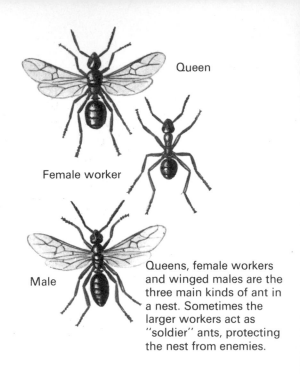

Queen

Female worker

Male

Queens, female workers and winged males are the three main kinds of ant in a nest. Sometimes the larger workers act as "soldier" ants, protecting the nest from enemies.

## What is an ant nursery?

Ants live and work in nests under the ground. Some nests are homes for thousands of ants. There are three main kinds of ants in a nest, each with a special job to do.

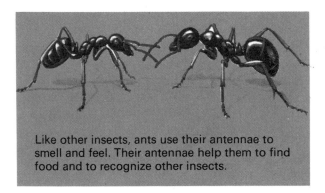

Like other insects, ants use their antennae to smell and feel. Their antennae help them to find food and to recognize other insects.

The largest ant is the queen. She spends most of her time laying eggs which will turn into new queens, female worker ants and male ants, which have wings. The female workers dig the nest and look after it. They gather food to bring back to the nest and look after the eggs and young ants. The male ants mate with the new queen ants but do no work in the nest.

When it is time to mate, the queen grows wings and leaves the nest with the males for mating. This is called the marriage flight. When she returns to the nest she looses her wings and begins to lay her eggs. She lays them in a special room in the nest called the royal chamber. Workers carry the eggs to a nursery chamber where they will hatch into larvae.

The larvae grow and turn into pupae. The workers move them again, this time into pupae chambers, where they will become adult ants. Other rooms in the nest are used for storing food and rubbish.

INSIDE AN ANTS' NEST

Hunting

Pupae chamber

Royal chamber

## How do ants "farm"?

Many ants look after small insects called aphids. The aphids give the ants food. The ants stroke the aphids until they give out a sweet juice called honeydew, which the ants love to eat. In fact, they "milk" the aphids, just as a farmer milks his herd of dairy cows. Some ants will even protect the aphids by building shelters over them. Others dig out "stables" around aphids that feed on roots underground.

Leaf-cutter ants use nest chambers for growing a special kind of fungus which they feed to their young. They grow fungus just as a farmer grows crops.

Driver ants, sometimes called Army or Soldier ants, live in hot countries. Sometimes thousands march across the land, eating anything in their path.

Farming aphids

Nursery chamber

Food store

Digging

Pupae chamber

Rubbish room

# All About Birds

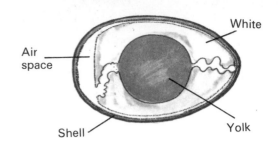

## How do birds' eggs hatch?

Inside an egg, as you can see from the picture on the right, there are the yolk, the white, and thick strands to keep the yolk in place. The yolk is the food for the growing chick.

The chick begins as a tiny spot in the yolk. Air can pass through the shell to the growing chick, and the air space inside is used by it just before it hatches out.

Eggs must be kept warm and safe from cracks or breaks. The chick takes in food from the yolk, and the white part slowly dries up. Soon, the chick grows as big as its shell. It must break out of the shell to keep on growing. Baby chicks have a tiny tooth at the end of their beaks. They use this tooth to break through the shell. The tooth breaks off as the chick pushes through the hole.

A newly-hatched chick is wet, and tired from its work. But it soon dries out, and looks forward to its first outdoor meal!

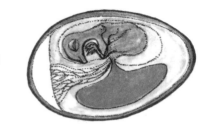

The chicken hatches

## Why do birds have feathers?

A bird's feathers keep it warm and dry, and help it to fly well. Birds today have more feathers and longer wings than the very first birds had. Their wings are strong, and each feather has a special job to do. When a bird moves its wings, its wing feathers open and close. This helps the bird to lift itself off the ground, and to stay in the air while it flies. Some birds do not flap their wings all the time. Instead, they use air currents to lift and move them. This is called gliding. Some birds can glide for hundreds of kilometres.

## Do all birds have beaks and claws?

All birds have beaks, but not all of them have claws. Some birds have webbed feet instead, like the mallard duck in the picture below. These act as paddles for the duck when it swims through the water. Claws would not be nearly as useful for a swimming bird.

Although all birds have beaks, their beaks are very different from each other. This is because the birds live very different sorts of lives, and need to do a whole variety of things. Hawks, like the one above, have curved sharp beaks. These help the hawk to grab its prey quickly, and hold on to it securely. The stork above has a long, sharp beak. This is useful for grabbing fish from the water. The stork may also need to toss the fish in the air and catch it again in a better way. Their beak helps with this, too. Woodpeckers have long sharp beaks too, but for a different reason. Woodpeckers need them because they peck into trees for insects and mites.

## What is the most common bird?

The sparrow is the most common bird in the world today. It does not have any unusual features. Its beak is wide and short, and its claws are small. But it can live and breed almost anywhere, both in the country and in towns and cities. This means that the modern world does not threaten the sparrow. Not many birds have done as well.

# Birds' Nests

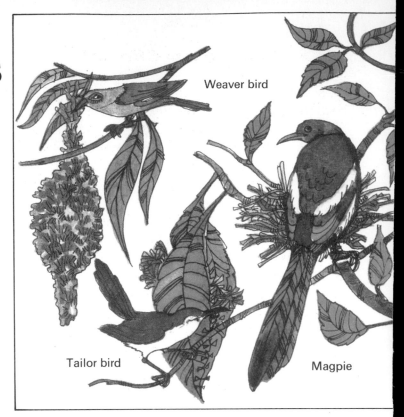

Weaver bird

Tailor bird

Magpie

## What do birds use to build their nests?

A lot of different things are used in nest building. Mud, dried grasses and twigs are the most common, but many birds also use feathers, leaves and moss. Some small birds use the webs of spiders to hold everything tightly together.

Birds mostly use whatever is close by – seagulls often use seaweed. But some birds will fly miles for the right materials.

## What shapes are used for nests?

The picture above shows just three of the shapes used for nests, but there are many others. A round or oval shape is the most common one, but some birds build nests which are almost entirely flat. The tailor bird's nest is a bit like an envelope. It sews two or three leaves together with grass, and then fills the space in the middle with soft, warm moss.

## How long does a nest take to build?

Some birds build their nests in just a few hours, while others take days to construct.

One nest that takes a long time to build is the weaver bird's. The stages in the nest building are shown in the pictures below.

First, the weaver bird gathers enough dried grass for the job. Then it chooses just the right twigs for the frame. You can see how the bird begins to wind the grasses around the twigs. When they are covered, the weaver bird adds pieces across the width as well. The finished nest has only a tiny space left. The parent birds use this to come and go.

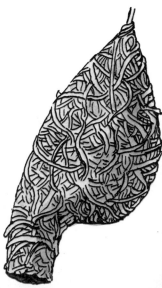

## Why are birds' nests so different?

American robin

The sort of nest a bird builds depends on the sort of place it lives in, and what sort of eggs it lays. A few birds – such as the Emperor penguin – do not build a nest at all. Instead, the penguins take turns to hold the eggs between their feet and their bodies, to keep them warm and safe. But most birds use nests to protect their eggs. They build them in trees and bushes, and on the ground.

Plovers build their nest on the ground. The male plover turns round and round in the sand, until it has made a dip in the ground with its movement. Then the female plover lines the dip with shells and stones. The eggs look like stones themselves, and they are very hard to see.

Some seabirds nest on cliffs. Their nests are often shallow and made just from twigs, because their eggs are a special shape. They do not need to be stopped from rolling off the cliff. The eggs are pear-shaped, and just roll in a small circle.

The reed warbler makes its nest in the reeds where it lives. Its nest is strong and sturdy, and is hung between the reeds. It cannot be easily seen.

Reed warbler

## How often do birds build nests?

Most birds build a new nest each year. Swallows, however, often return to the same nest from year to year. Birds build a nest when they are ready to lay their eggs and rear a family. The nest keeps the eggs and the young birds safe from harm, until they are ready to fly and can look after themselves.

Hummingbird

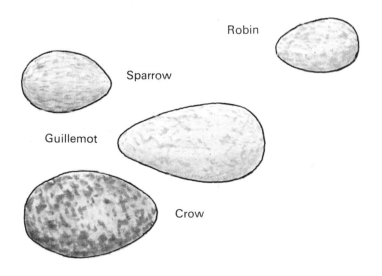

Robin

Sparrow

Guillemot

Crow

Lapwing

# On the Seashore

Puffin

Herring gull

Cormorant

Gannet

Black headed gull

Oyster catcher

Seal

Prawn

Scallop

Mussels

Limpet

Crab

Goby

Sea urchin

Sea anemone

Barnacles

Hermit Crab

An empty, windswept beach may seem a lonely place. But the seashore is home for many different creatures, both on land and in the sea. Some, like mussels and barnacles live out of the water at low tide. They have ways of keeping their bodies from drying out until the tide comes in again. Other creatures such as cockles and clams burrow under the sand when the tide is out.

Starfish

Cockle

### Is the sea anemone a flower?

Sea anemones look rather like the flower of the anemone plant. But they are a kind of animal without a skeleton. They cling to rocks under the sea or in rock pools at low tide. Anemones "open" like flowers and wave their tentacles about to catch food. When danger threatens they can close up again.

### Where does the hermit crab get its name?

A hermit crab hides away from other sea creatures. It spends its life in the empty shell of a whelk or other sea snail. The shell protects the hermit crab. Hermit crabs walk along the sea bed carrying their "homes" on their back. But they do not always live alone. Some hermit crabs have sea anemones attached to their shells. The crab helps the anemone by carrying it to where there is food. The anemone helps the hermit crab too. The crab gets the "leftovers" from food the anemone catches.

### Do cormorants dry themselves off?

Cormorants are diving birds that live near the sea. They usually only enter the water for fishing, because their feathers get wet easily. A bird cannot fly well with wet feathers. When a cormorant returns from a fishing expedition, it will often stand on a rock with its wings stretched out sideways. This helps to dry the feathers out quickly.

### Do starfish have feet?

We usually call the points of a starfish its "arms". But underneath each arm are rows of tiny tube-feet. These feet are like tiny suckers which help the starfish to move over the sea bottom. Some starfish use their tube-feet to pull open the shells of mussels.

### What do puffins and rabbits have in common?

Puffins are short, stubby seabirds that live along cliff tops. They nest in burrows under the ground. Often a puffin will take over a deserted rabbit burrow to nest in. For hundreds of years puffins were caught for food by people living in the Scottish islands. In the Faeroes they are still caught in special scoops shaped like lacrosse sticks. The puffins are scooped up as they fly past.

# Under the Sea

**Is the sea horse a horse?**

The sea horse is a fish, not a horse. It gets its name from the shape of its head, which looks like the head of a horse. The sea horse swims upright and uses its tail to hold onto seaweed. It is unusual in another way, too. The male sea horse has a pouch, rather like a kangaroo's, into which the female lays her eggs. The male looks after the eggs until they are ready to hatch. A large male sometimes gives birth to as many as 400 young.

**Do flatfish lie on their sides?**

Flatfish such as plaice and flounder start their lives by swimming like other fish. Their eyes are on either side of their head. Then a strange thing happens. Gradually, a flatfish's eye moves across to the other side of its head. Its mouth also changes shape so that it is mostly on the same side of the head as the eyes. When both its eyes are on the same side of its head, the flatfish settles into the sea bed. It lies on its "blind" side, which stays white. Its upper side changes colour to match the sea floor.

**Are a lobster's claws all the same?**

A lobster has ten legs. The first two legs have become huge claws at the front of its body. But if you look closely, you will see that each of these claws is quite different from the other. One is heavy and thick and is used for crushing food. The other is longer and more delicate and has ridged "teeth". It is used for picking and scraping flesh off bones or shells. The male lobster's claws are much bigger than those of the female.

**Which fish is a fisherman?**

An angler fish uses a "rod" and "bait" to catch its dinner. Part of its *dorsal* (back) fin is very long and hangs out over the fish's mouth like a fishing rod. At the top of the fin is a tiny flap that looks like bait. Small fish attracted by the wriggling "bait" are snapped up into the angler fish's huge jaws.

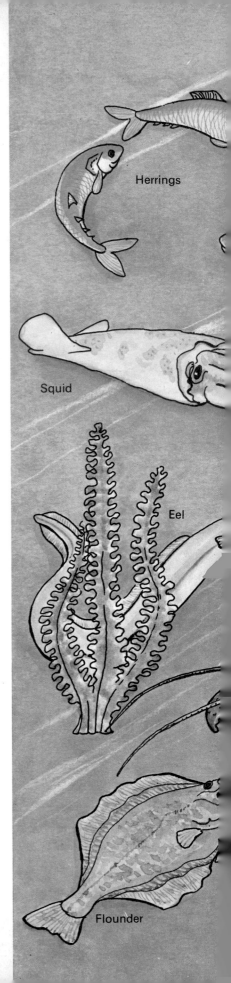

Herrings

Squid

Eel

Flounder

Sea horse

Pipefish

Spotted dogfish

Mackerel

Octopus

Lobster

Angler fish

Skate

Cod

## Can flying fish really fly?

Flying fish do indeed fly. But they are more like gliders than aeroplanes, because they can only fly short distances. A flying fish has specially long *pectoral* (chest) fins which it spreads out like wings to glide over the waves. Its body is streamlined like the body of a glider.

When a flying fish breaks the surface of the water, it uses its tail to "taxi" along the surface. Some flying fish reach speeds of 56 kilometres an hour before lifting themselves into the air. Free of the water, they can fly for up to half a minute and cover 400 metres. Scientists think that these fish "fly" mainly to escape danger under the water.

## Will an octopus drown a diver?

Some octopuses reach a length of $5\frac{1}{2}$ metres across their arms, but most are much smaller. They are also very shy, and will stay hidden or move away quickly if a diver comes near them. Because of this, they are not really dangerous to divers. But an octopus could hold a person under water long enough to drown him, especially if it were anchored firmly to a rock. This kind of accident does not happen very often.

## Can you write with octopus ink?

Inside the body of an octopus is a sac filled with ink. When the octopus is disturbed, it

Different sea creatures live at different depths. Animals such as jellyfish stay near the surface. Sea anemones and octopuses prefer the sea floor where the ocean is fairly shallow. Some animals, such as squid, are found in shallow and very deep waters.

Flying fish

Jellyfish

Shoal of herring

Tunny fish

Shrimps

Squid

Eel

Sea anemone

Octopus

Manta ray

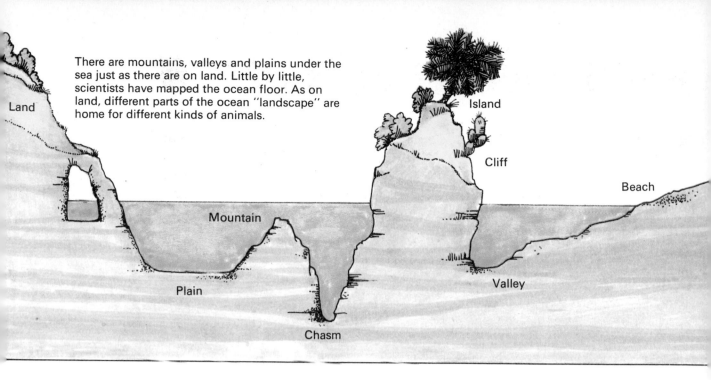

There are mountains, valleys and plains under the sea just as there are on land. Little by little, scientists have mapped the ocean floor. As on land, different parts of the ocean "landscape" are home for different kinds of animals.

Land

Island

Cliff

Beach

Mountain

Plain

Valley

Chasm

squirts the ink into the water. The ink hangs in the water like a black cloud and hides the octopus while it escapes. Octopus ink is called *sepia*. It has been used for hundreds of years for writing and drawing.

## How far do eels travel?

The Common eel lives in rivers and streams in Europe and America. When it is time to lay eggs these eels swim thousands of miles to the Sargasso Sea in the Atlantic Ocean. There they lay their eggs and die. When the young eels hatch, they begin the long swim to their parents' freshwater homes. The young of European eels take three years to make the trip "home".

## Is a jellyfish a fish?

A jellyfish is not a fish. Jellyfish belong to the group of animals that do not have backbones, called *invertebrates*. Fish have bony skeletons with backbones. They belong to the group of animals called *vertebrates*. People are vertebrates. If we did not have skeletons, we would be floppy like jellyfish.

How does a herring grow up?

A female herring lays thousands of eggs or spawn.

The eggs hatch into larvae.

The larvae swim near the shore and turn into whitebait.

A herring is fully grown when it is 1–2 years old.

# What do They Eat?

Monkey

Oryx

Panda

## Which animals eat plants?

Animals that eat plants are called *herbivores*. Their teeth and stomachs are well suited to the leaves, grass and fruit they eat. Monkeys have long, nimble fingers for picking fruit. Giraffes have long necks so they can eat leaves from the tops of trees. Some animals, like bears, are *omnivores*: they eat a bit of everything. But pandas eat only a special kind of bamboo. If they cannot find just the right sort, they will not eat anything else. That is one reason why pandas are scarce.

Lion

Eagle

Crocodile

Herring

Fox

Bear

## Who eats meat?

All the animals on the left eat meat. Animals that eat only meat are called *carnivores*. Such animals have special teeth for chewing up meat, and their stomachs can sort out the goodness from the fur, bones and other waste bits.

Eagles, like other birds of prey, eat smaller birds whole. They also eat small *rodents* like mice. Herring eat other smaller fish, and crocodiles eat fish as well. Foxes like eating meat best, but like bears they eat other foods as well. Bears like eating sweet fruit.

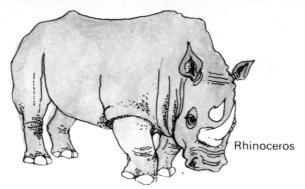
Rhinoceros

## How much to animals eat? How often do they eat?

A big plant-eating animal has to spend a lot of time eating, because it has to have at least as much food as it weighs, every day. This means that horses, zebras and other herbivores eat almost all day, if they can find enough grass.

In the wild, many carnivores do not eat every day. Lions and tigers often hunt and kill their prey one day, and then rest with full stomachs for another day or two before looking for more. The same thing happens with smaller carnivores. But when such animals are in zoos, or have become tame and are pets, they usually eat every day. An adult lion needs about 10 kilos of meat a day.

## When do animals hunt for their food?

Animals hunt at different times of the day and night. Some hunt only in the daytime – most herbivores use daylight to help them find their food. Others, like rabbits, look for food at dawn and dusk rather than in the full daylight. This helps them hide from their enemies.

Carnivores like cats often hunt at night, for their eyes are large and they can use moonlight to seek for food. Owls, too, are carnivores. They sleep in the daytime and hunt at night. Their eyes are specially made to see straight ahead, and this is best for hunting animals. They can also hear very well. They look and listen for small animals like mice, and then they can easily pounce and catch them.

An owl eats a lot of food in one year. Look at the chart on the right to see the different animals it eats.

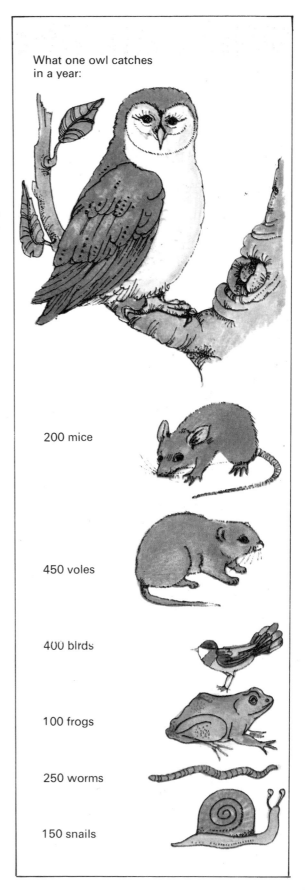
What one owl catches in a year:

200 mice

450 voles

400 birds

100 frogs

250 worms

150 snails

# All Sorts of Dogs

## Why are there so many different breeds of dog?

There are hundreds of different breeds of dog, and two main reasons for this. One of the reasons lies in the history of dogs. Thousands of years ago, all the dogs in the world were wild. As the different groups of dogs developed, some became tame. People used these dogs to hunt for food, and others became pet dogs and lived with families.

These different groups of dogs lived in different parts of the world. All our modern breeds developed from these wild dogs. One group is called the Northern Group. Sheepdogs and alsatians belong to this group, which probably began with the large grey wolves which lived in Europe. Another group is called the Mastiff Group, and these dogs are all famous for having a very keen sense of smell. Basset hounds and dalmatians belong to this group.

The other reason for so many different breeds has been caused by people. Many people are very interested in special dog breeds, and enjoy developing these. This means that new breeds are appearing almost every year. Some are just small, or *miniature*, versions of existing ones, while others are completely new.

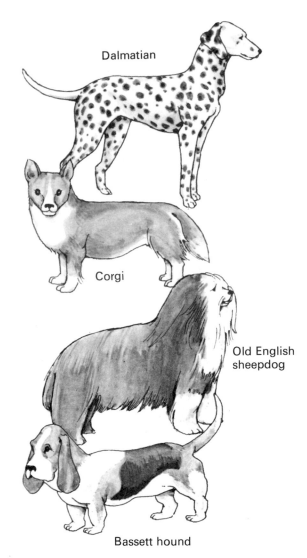

Dalmatian

Corgi

Old English sheepdog

Bassett hound

## Why do people own dogs?

Lots of people enjoy keeping a dog as a pet. Dog-lovers say they are clever, friendly and good companions – and dogs have long been called "man's best friend" because of their loyalty to their owners. Many people do not want to own a special breed of dog. They are happy to have a *mongrel* – a dog that is a mixture of different breeds. Some owners say that mongrels are the cleverest of all the dogs!

But dogs are used for lots of jobs, too.

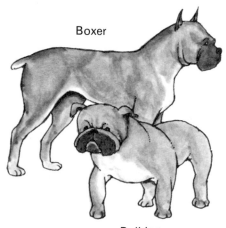

Boxer

Bulldog

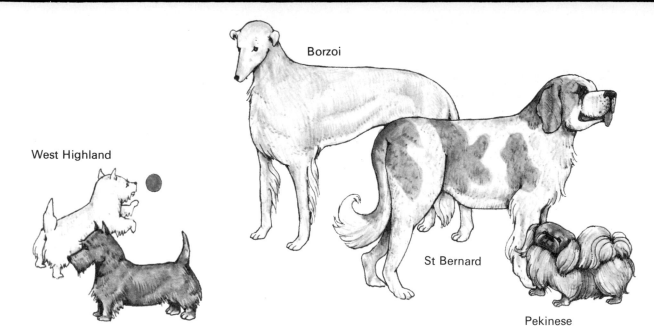

West Highland

Borzoi

St Bernard

Pekinese

Many dogs lead hard-working lives herding sheep, guiding blind people, and hunting. Other dogs are used by the police to help track down criminals. Some dogs are better at these tasks than others, so they are bred just for the work they do.

Some sorts of dogs were bred to do a job of work, but are no longer used for it. They are just kept as pets, instead. Terriers like the ones above were bred to hunt rabbits and rats. Collies were used to herd sheep, goats and cows. Borzois were hunting dogs, which chased after wild animals. Of all those dogs, it is really only the sheep dogs which are still bred for the work they do.

### How long do dogs live?

This varies from breed to breed. A dog is grown-up when it is one year old, and some dogs may live to be 20 years old, or even older. But most dogs live only about 12 years.

### How big can dogs grow?

An adult miniature dog can be as small as 120 mm from toe to shoulder, and a big dog like an Irish wolfhound might grow to be

1 m tall. It is hard to tell how tall a dog will grow if it is a mongrel. If it has big paws, it will probably grow to match them!

### How is a new breed made?

Some dogs have been bred from older kinds which no longer exist. The bull dog was first used for a cruel sport called bull-baiting. When that was outlawed, the original bulldog was crossbred with a terrier to make a bull terrier. Modern bulldogs and boxers are heavy, strong dogs with very powerful jaws. The boxer is partly bulldog, partly some German breeds of dog.

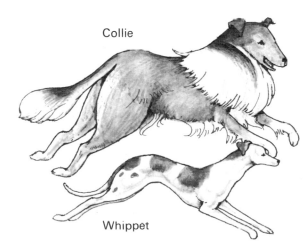

Collie

Whippet

# Big and Small Cats

## How are cats different from other animals?

Members of the cat family are called *felines*. They are all meat-eaters, and they catch the animals they eat by *stalking* them. Cats have good eyesight, and an excellent sense of smell. Using these aids, they creep silently towards the animal without being noticed. When they are close enough, the cats spring out from cover and pounce on their prey. Some cats can run very fast over a short distance. They use this skill in hunting.

All cats have short muzzles, long sleek bodies, and curving claws. Most cats have claws that *retract* back into their paws when they are not in use. Cats use their claws for climbing, and fighting.

Cats cannot see in complete darkness, but they can see in the smallest gleam of light. This means they can hunt at night.

## When did cats first become tame?

No one is sure when this happened, but cats have been kept as pets for at least three thousand years. The ancient Egytians tamed cats, and at first used them for hunting. Later on, cats were also kept as pets by the Egyptians. These people thought cats were very special. They worshipped them in their *temples*, had cat gods, and carved statues of cats. When a family's pet cat died, the whole family shaved their eyebrows to show their unhappiness!

Many other countries have kept cats as pets for a long time. In China, India and Japan cats were valued for their killing of rats and mice. The Romans brought pet cats with them to Britain.

At some stages in history, cats have been thought to be unlucky or even evil, but today many people enjoy their company. There are lots of different pet cats to choose from.

Lion

Leopard

Puma

Tiger

Serval

House cat

Lynx

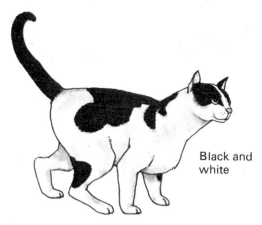

Black and
white

Tortoiseshell

## What are the different breeds?

There are many different kinds of cats, divided into two groups: those with long hair, and those with short hair. The chinchilla on the right is a popular breed of long haired cat. Chinchillas are all the same colour, but long haired cats come in many different colours, from black, tabby, brown and red to a bluey grey and white.

Chinchilla

There are more different breeds of short haired cats than of long haired ones. Most ordinary cats which do not belong to any special breed have short hair. They are often tabby, with different sorts of stripes in their coats. Siamese cats are a famous breed of short haired cat. Their coats are dark only at the "points" of head, tail and paws; the rest of their coats are pale. Their bodies are sleek and long, and they have bright blue eyes.

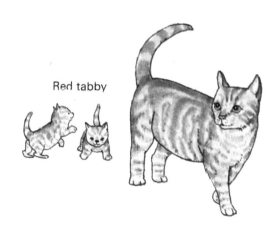

Red tabby

Many people are interested in foreign breeds of cats, like the Siamese, Burmese, Abyssinian, and so on. There are different varieties to choose from among these, too, for they now come in different colours. Cats like this are taken to shows and compete for prizes. They often cost a lot of money to buy.

But ordinary cats are very popular too. They make good pets, especially for people without space to keep a dog, and they are interesting to watch. Even domestic cats sometimes behave like their relations the lions and tigers.

Siamese

Cream
Burmese

# Horses and Ponies

A galloping horse

## What is the difference between a horse and a pony?

The only real difference is one of size. Both ponies and horses are members of the same family of animals, but ponies are smaller. Most ponies do not grow taller than 14 hands (142 cm), and Shetland ponies are much smaller than that. Their height limit is less than 10 hands (95 cm).

Piebald riding horse

Shetland pony

Arab horse

## Are there any wild horses left?

The only wild horses known to exist in the world today live in zoos. All breeds of horse began from wild herds, and those horses which live on open land now behave as their *ancestors* did. They gather in groups and are constantly moving around to find new grass to eat. Each group, or herd, is led by a male horse, called a *stallion*. The stallion protects the rest of the herd from danger. Female horses are called *mares*. Their babies are called *colts* if they are male, and *fillies* if they are female.

## How many horses are there today? What are they used for?

There are about 65 million horses in the world now, although it is not long since there were almost twice that number. Horses used to be used for a lot of heavy work on farms and in towns. It is only in the last 100 years that machines have taken their place.

Even now there are many working horses. Police use them to control crowds, and some small farms still employ horses instead of tractors. The rounding up of cattle on big South American farms is still done from horseback. But most horses are kept for pleasure, by their owners. Riding is a very popular sport, although it is also quite expensive.

## What animals are related to horses?

Donkeys, asses and zebras are all members of the same family. But the rhinoceros, surprisingly, is a close relation too!

## What are the most famous breeds?

Many breeds of horse have been improved by using an Arab horse at some stage. Arabs are famous for their beauty and speed, and they are also very strong. Race horses have all been bred from Arabs.

Palaminos and Appaloosa horses began in America, but both are now popular all over the world. Palominos are a golden colour, but Appaloosas are covered with brown or black spots.

British breeds, like Exmoor and New Forest ponies, are often used as children's riding ponies.

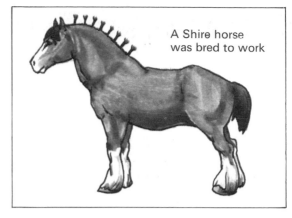

A Shire horse was bred to work

Above: The Shire horse is one of the biggest heavy horses in the world. Horses like this can grow to be two metres tall, and weigh more than one tonne. Only an elephant is stronger than an adult Shire horse, of all the animals which are used by people to do pulling work.

Below: The equipment used on horses when they are ridden is always much the same. A bridle and saddle are the best way for a rider to control the horse, and to be comfortable while doing so. This bridle and saddle are very simple; some are much more complicated than these, with special bits, double reins, and high pommels.

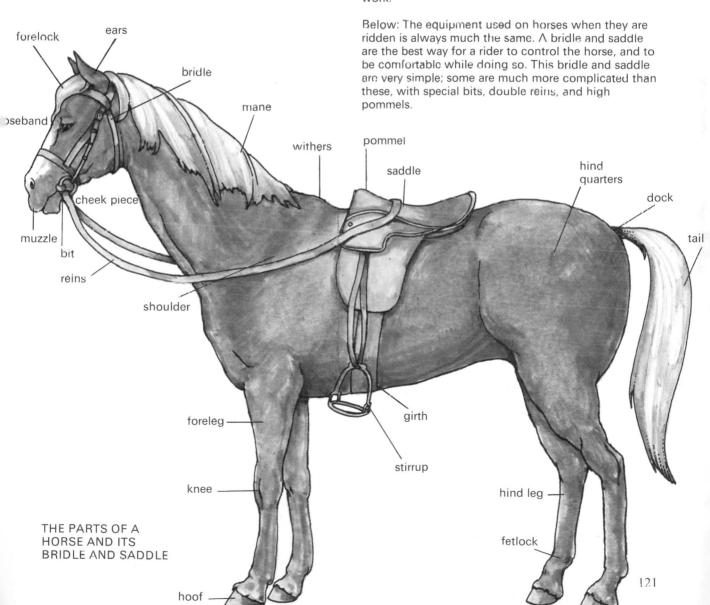

THE PARTS OF A HORSE AND ITS BRIDLE AND SADDLE

121

# Animals that Work for Us

### Are there dolphins in the navy?

Dolphins, like whales, are mammals. They are very intelligent and easy to train. Many dolphins are kept in aquaria where they entertain people with their tricks. Scientists have been able to study dolphins in aquaria. They know now that dolphins can find their way or locate things under water by using their own type of "sonar". Like

make us laugh. Chimpanzees can be trained to behave like people and are funny to watch. To be good performers, animals must be well looked after and kindly treated. They often enjoy their work and seem to know when they have done well.

### Do insects work for people?

Many insects are helpful to us. The best known are the bees. People keep bees for

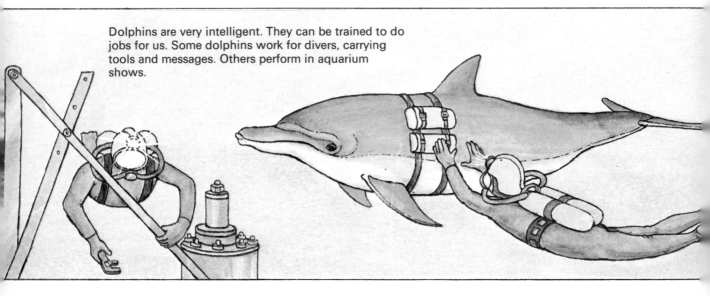

Dolphins are very intelligent. They can be trained to do jobs for us. Some dolphins work for divers, carrying tools and messages. Others perform in aquarium shows.

the sonar on a ship or submarine, the dolphins' sonar picks up echoes from sounds bounced off objects in the water.

Some dolphins have joined the U.S. Navy. Because they are so easy to train, they are used by navy divers to carry tools and messages, and for finding things under the water.

### Which animals make us laugh?

Many animals are easy to train. They can be taught to do many tricks. In a circus, seals, monkeys and dancing bears often

making honey. The bees live in special hives put there for them by the beekeeper. They gather nectar, a sweet liquid, from flowers and take it to the hive. There they make it into honey in honeycombs. The beekeeper looks after the hives and removes the honeycombs when they are full. He must wear special clothing, gloves and headgear to protect him from bee stings.

Insects are helpful to man in other ways, too. Ladybirds eat garden pests, such as greenfly. Silkworms, which give us silk, are the larvae of silk moths. A red dye called cochineal comes from an insect that lives on prickly pear cactus.

Depending on where in the world they live, people use different animals for carrying heavy loads.

Camel     Reindeer     Llama     Yak

People keep bees for the honey they make. The bees live in special hives. The top of each hive lifts off so that the beekeeper can take out the honeycombs.

## Why is the camel a good desert worker?

Camels are well suited to the hot deserts. They can go for a long time without water. People used to think that camels stored water in their humps. This is not true. Camels cannot store water. But they do not lose water from their bodies as easily as we do. Camels do not perspire until they are very hot indeed. They will actually huddle together to keep cool! This is because the heat from their bodies is cooler than the heat from the Sun. Huddled together, a smaller part of each camel's body is exposed to the Sun's heat.

The water buffalo pulls a plough in a rice field in India. These huge animals are very strong but quite gentle when they are trained.

Cart horse

Guide dog

## What do they give us?

Sheep give us wool and meat.

Chickens give us meat and eggs.

Cattle give us meat and milk.

Yaks give meat, milk and skins.

## How do elephants work for us?

There are two main kinds of elephant, the African elephant and the Indian elephant. Almost all trained elephants are Indian elephants. They are gentler and easier to teach. In India and South-east Asia, elephants work in the forests. They carry huge logs with their trunk. Some elephants work in circuses.

Elephants were once used in armies. In the 200s BC Hannibal, a famous general, used elephants to fight the Romans. But the Romans thought of a way to beat them back. As the elephants charged, the Romans blew on trumpets and strewed the ground with spikes. The elephants were terrified, and turned back, trampling some of Hannibal's own men.

## Why is the dog "man's best friend"?

A happy pet dog may be a good friend. But dogs can be friends in other ways too. Many dogs do important jobs for people. Police dogs help the police in many kinds of detective work. Huskies in northern Canada and Alaska are strong workers, pulling sledges for many miles over the snow. Guide dogs help the blind to find their way. Guard dogs protect homes, warehouses and other buildings from intruders.

Huskies

Elephant

Donkey

Cat

Above: All these animals work for people. Each one has a very special job to do.

## Can birds "go fishing" for us?

Cormorants are expert diving birds. Their long necks, long bodies and webbed feet make them good swimmers. For hundreds of years, cormorants have fished for people in China and Japan. They are trained to dive for fish from a boat and return with their catch. A long string tied to each cormorant guides it back to the boat, and a ring around its neck prevents it from swallowing the fish. Today, people still fish with comorants in China, but in Japan it is just for tourists to watch.

Cormorants help with fishing in China and Japan. Each bird has a ring around its neck to keep it from swallowing the fish it catches.

# Animals on the Farm

Bull

Cow

Calf

Sow

Cock

Piglet

Dog

Chicks

Ducks

Hen

Pigs give us:

Pork

Bacon

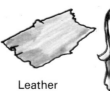

Leather

Cows give us:

Milk

Mare

Foal

Stallion

Lamb

Ram

Ewe

## Why do we keep pigs?

Today we mostly keep pigs for their meat – ham and pork. But hundreds of years ago pigs had other jobs to do. The ancient Egyptians used pigs to tread the wheat they had sown into the ground. Pigs were once used for rounding up cattle and for finding *truffles*, a fungus delicacy which grows under the ground. Pigs are good at clearing ground, too. They root for food, turning over the soil with their snouts and eat small plants, fruits and nuts as they go.

## How long have chickens been kept for food?

We know that over 5000 years ago chickens were kept for food by people living in India. Today many chickens are raised on *battery farms*. They are kept indoors and are fed special chicken feed. After only three months the chickens are big enough to be sold. Chickens also give us eggs. Battery eggs come from chickens raised on feed indoors. Free range eggs come from chickens which live outside and eat insects, seeds and worms.

## How much wool does one sheep give us?

There are many different kinds, or breeds, of sheep. Some are kept for wool, some for meat, others for wool and meat. One kind of sheep in New Zealand gives up to 10 kilograms of wool, or fleece, in one year. Others may give only 3 or 4 kilograms a year. Most sheep are sheared once or twice a year.

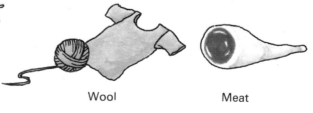

Meat     Leather     Sheep give us:     Wool     Meat

# How Does a Plant Grow?

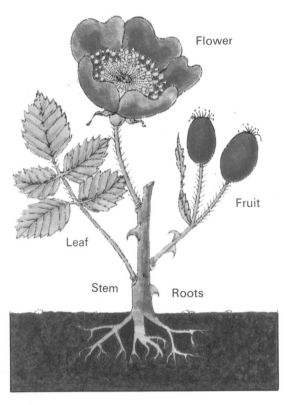

Flower

Fruit

Leaf

Stem

Roots

few parts. It does not have roots or flowers, so it has just a few different sorts of cells. But other plants have roots, shoots and leaves. They might have about 80 different sorts of cells.

There are three main parts in plants like the one on the left: the roots, the shoots and the leaves. The roots seek out water and minerals from the soil, and pass these on to the shoots. Roots are also the anchor for the plant, and keep it firm in the ground. The main shoot of a plant is its stem. This carries the water and minerals to the leaves, and holds up the leaves and flowers.

The plant's leaves store and make food. Most other plant parts have developed from these three parts. Flowers, for instance, have developed from leaves.

## What parts does a plant have?

All the parts of a plant are made from cells. Most cells are so tiny, they can be seen only through a microscope. Each cell contains special chemicals, and these are what decide what work the cell will do. Some plant cells, for example, store food while others are used to carry water around to leaves.

Some plants have more parts than others. A very simple plant, like *algae*, has only a

## What is seed germination?

A seed *germinates* when it starts to grow. Germination begins when the seed takes in water from the soil, swells, and bursts through its seed coat. The main root comes out first, and then the main shoot.

The seed has enough food inside the seed coat to nourish the seedling plant until the first leaves are formed.

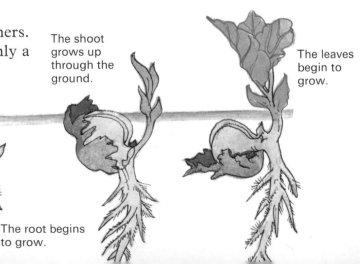

The shoot grows up through the ground.

The leaves begin to grow.

The seed is buried in the ground.

It splits open.

The root begins to grow.

## How do seeds feed themselves?

A growing seed needs food to help it grow, but it has no roots to bring water and minerals. So seeds have food packed inside their seed coat with the tiny grain which germinates. This grain uses the food until it is big enough to make its own food.

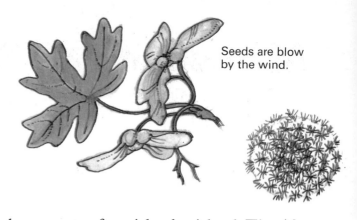

Seeds are blow by the wind.

## How do seeds travel?

When a plant produces its seeds, that is just the beginning of the story. Each seed needs to leave its parent plant and find a good place to grow. There it can germinate and turn into a new plant. Plants use a lot of different ways to spread their seeds around the land.

Seeds fall on the ground.

They are carried by birds.

One of the most common ways used to spread seeds is by the wind. Plants such as dandelions have tiny hairs attached to each seed. These hairs act like parachutes for the seed, and carry it a long way in even a light breeze.

Some plants produce their seeds in pods. When the pods are ripe and the seeds are ready, the pods burst open. This explosion forces the seeds out into the air, and they can fly for quite a long way.

Plants which grow near water often produce seeds which can float. These are carried by the river or stream to distant fields, where they will grow. Coconuts, the biggest seeds in the world, are often carried by sea water, from island to island. The tide washes the coconuts up onto beaches. There they may take root and grow into a new coconut palm.

## How do animals help?

Animals often help to move seeds around, although they do not know what they are doing. Some seeds have sticky hairs or hooks on them. These will stick to the fur of any animal that brushes past, and the animal will carry the seed with it until it is knocked off again. Squirrels bury acorns and other nuts for a winter food store, but they sometimes forget where the store is. The forgotten nuts may sprout in the springtime, especially if they have been buried underneath a pile of rotting leaves.

Birds often carry seeds far away from the parent plant. They may fly with them to a nest, or a safe place, and drop them on the way. Seeds which birds and animals eat will eventually be left on the ground, too, in the animal's droppings.

Seeds are carried by animals.

# More About Plants

### What do seeds look like?

Plants which have flowers *reproduce* themselves by making seeds. Inside each seed is a tiny grain, called an *embryo*. This will grow, and after a while it will become a new plant itself.

The embryo needs food while it grows, and seeds have food stores which the embryo can use. Many of these food stores are eaten by animals, including human ones, as part of their diet.

The picture on the right shows a lot of different seeds. Some fruit, like tomatoes, have lots of seeds inside them. The head of a poppy flower has a seed case. This dries when the flower dies, and the seeds are blown by the wind. Poppy seeds are no bigger than the head of a pin.

Other seeds come singly, or in twos or threes. Acorns are single seeds, and are a kind of nut. Beans have their seeds inside a case called a *pod*. A pod may contain up to six or eight separate seeds. Peas have their seeds arranged in the same way as beans.

### Why do plants have flowers?

The flowers of a plant have a very important job to do. They produce and protect the seeds, and make sure the seeds are *fertilised* so they can grow.

Some plants use the wind to blow a special powder called *pollen* onto the flowers. The pollen fertilises a part of the plant called the *stigma*. Plants that use wind for this job have tiny flowers with small petals. This makes sure nothing gets in the way of the pollen. Other plants use bees, not wind.

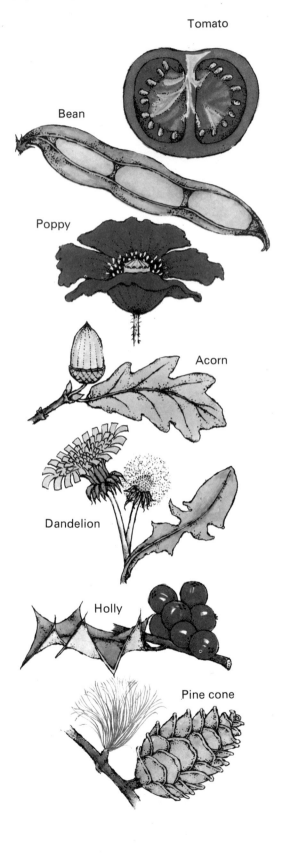

Tomato

Bean

Poppy

Acorn

Dandelion

Holly

Pine cone

## How do roots work?

When a seed first sprouts and begins to grow, the main root is the first part to appear. After a time its branches, and other smaller roots are formed as well. The growth of the roots keeps pace with the needs of the plant.

Roots have tubes inside them. All these tubes meet up with a central bunch of tubes in the stem of the plant. These carry water and food around the plant to the growing parts.

The outside skin of the roots is covered with a network of tiny root hairs. It is these which draw water from the soil for the plant to use. The root hairs do not live for very long. They are soon replaced by new hairs. But the main root continues to grow and flourish. A plant can usually survive if its root hairs are cut off, and even if some of its smaller roots are damaged. But if a plant's main root is cut, it will die. It cannot get the water and food that it needs to stay alive.

## What are runners?

Some plants reproduce themselves by runners instead of seeds. The runners are long stems. They root into the ground, and new baby plants grow from these. Strawberry plants grow from runners.

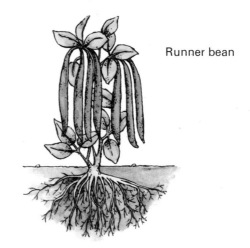

Runner bean

Many fibrous roots

Dandelion

Big tap root

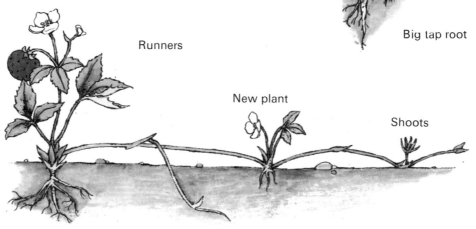

Runners

New plant

Shoots

Strawberry plant

# Plants from Bible Lands

A cedar tree

The flag of Lebanon

### Why is there a tree on Lebanon's flag?

The tree on Lebanon's flag is a cedar. It was cedar trees from Lebanon that Solomon used to build his wonderful temple. King Hiram from that country gave Solomon the trees. It took many years for thousands of men to chop down all the trees that were needed to build the temple.

### What is linen made from?

Linen is made from the stalks of the flax plant. It is the oldest kind of cloth that we know about. The ancient Egyptians wrapped their pharaohs in linen before they buried them in the pyramids. The old Hebrew priests wore linen.

Flax plants have blue flowers. Because it is strong, flax is also used to make rope and canvas.

## What is papyrus?

Papyrus is an Egyptian water plant that was used by the ancient Egyptians to make a kind of paper. The graceful plant grows from a metre to 3 metres high.

The paper made from the inside of the plant is also called papyrus. The plant was cut into strips. The strips were laid side by side. Then other strips were laid across these. The layers were stuck together and hammered flat. When the papyrus was dried in the sun it made a very good material for writing on.

Sheets of papyrus were joined into long strips and rolled as in the picture above.

Pieces of papyrus have been found that are thousands of years old.

Papyrus was also made into baskets, boats, sails and rope.

## Are there many different kinds of bread?

People eat bread in nearly every country. For thousands of years people have been crushing grain to a powder and mixing it with water or milk to make a dough.

But not all bread was or is the same. The Hebrew woman below is making un-leavened bread. Unleavened bread has no *yeast* in it. Yeast fills the bread with bubbles of gas which make it grow bigger. Most bread has yeast of some kind in it. The Hebrews baked their bread in thin sheets.

Bread can be made from many plants. It is made from barley, rye, oats, rice, potatoes and nuts. Most of our bread is made from wheat.

Weaving flax into cloth.

# More Bible Land Plants

### How do dates grow?

Dates grow on trees called *date palms*. There are many different kinds of palms, but they all look rather the same. Leaves sprout straight out of the top of the trunk. Date palm leaves are between 4 metres and 6 metres long. Palm trees grow in hot, dry countries.

Dates grow in big bunches of as many as 200. They are a rich red or golden colour when they are on the tree. The ones we usually eat have been dried.

The trunk and the leaves of the date palm are used by the Arabs for building houses and weaving rope and mats.

The date palm has been grown for its fruit for over 4000 years. Another well known palm is the coconut. The white inside of the coconut is made into oil to make soap and margarine.

Dates

Dried date

### What are grapes used for?

We eat red and white grapes. But do you know that when you eat raisins and currants you are also eating grapes that have been dried? Grapes, most of all, are used to make wine.

The *grape vine* has been grown by people for at least 3000 years. Seeds of grapes have been found in ancient Egyptian tombs.

There are many different kinds of grapes, some with seeds and some without, some white and some dark red, some sour, some sweet. They grow best in dry, sunny places. Because they are vines, grapes have to be tied to stakes. If they are looked after, grape vines may give fruit for over 300 years.

The countries which grow most grapes are Italy, France, Spain and Portugal. They are also grown in large quantities in the American state of California.

Grapes

Raisins

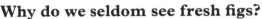
Figs

Dried fig

## Why do we seldom see fresh figs?

We seldom see juicy fresh figs because when they are taken from the tree they are very soft and *perishable*. They are so difficult to handle that they are usually dried in the sun. When the figs are dried they last for a long time.

Figs grow in warm lands. They are mentioned in the Bible and other old books.

Dried figs have a lot of sugar in them.

## Where do olives grow?

Olives grow mostly in countries around the Mediterranean Sea – Spain, Italy and Greece.

The olive tree grows very slowly, but it keeps growing for a very long time. In some places there are trees over 1000 years old. Unripe olives are green. As they ripen they turn purple and then black. Most olives are grown for the oil in them. Those that have to be made into oil are left on the trees until they are ripe. Then they are crushed and the olive oil squeezed out of them. About a quarter of the weight of an olive is oil.

Olive oil is used mostly in salad dressings and as cooking fat.

Ripe olives

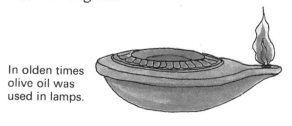

In olden times olive oil was used in lamps.

# All About Trees

## Do trees ever stop growing?

Animals stop growing when they reach the limit of their size, but plants keep growing as long as they are alive. Trees are a special sort of plant, because they have a woody stem. The tips of the trees' shoots and roots are the parts that grow the most, but the woody stem, called the trunk, also thickens as it grows. If a tree trunk is cut through, you can see rings in the wood called growth rings. These show how old the tree is, because a ring is added each year.

The leaves, buds and flowers of a tree always grow to a set pattern. This pattern is different for each sort of tree. It is very important that each leaf can get sunlight, and trees arrange for this to happen in different ways.

## How do the buds form? When do they open?

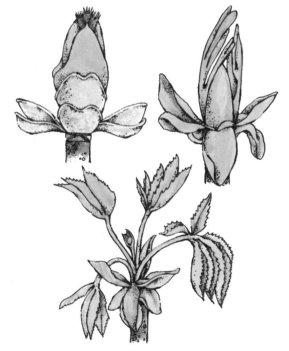

Before a bud of new leaves opens on a tree, the tiny leaves are already formed inside. The tree has started to develop these leaves long before spring comes.

When warm weather tells the tree that the winter is over, *sap* starts to rise in the trunk and spread to the branches. Sap is a thick, sticky liquid made by the tree as food. As the sap spreads, the leaves inside the buds swell and grow larger. The outer scales of the buds then fall away, and the new leaves are exposed to the sunlight and warmth. They slowly grow and stretch up and out to the sun.

It is quite easy to watch this happening for yourself. Pick a small budding twig from a tree in the springtime, like the horse chestnut twig on the left. Put this in a jar of water, and leave the jar on a sunny windowsill. The buds will open and grow, just as they would on the living tree.

## Why do trees have such different leaves?

Trees all need leaves for the same reason; the leaves make food. But trees also lose a lot of water through their leaves, and the bigger the leaves are, the more water they lose.

Trees that live in moist places have large leaves, for they can easily replace the water they lose. In cooler countries trees have smaller leaves, like the needles on pines. Some trees in cool countries lose their leaves in autumn, and do not make new ones till spring. This helps stop the tree losing too much water. The oak sheds its leaves, and so does the horse chestnut.

Oak

Scots pine

Horse chestnut

Willow

## Why do some leaves change colour in autumn?

This happens to trees that shed their leaves in autumn. As the leaves dry up, and before they fall from the tree, they often turn bright colours. The green colour is not being replaced, and the "real" colour of the leaves shows through.

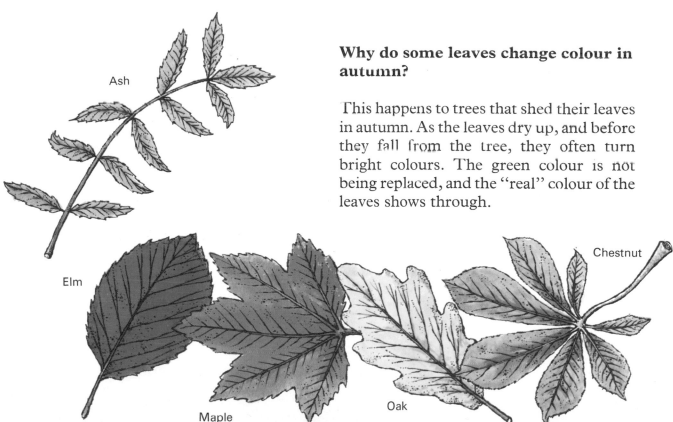

Ash

Elm

Maple

Oak

Chestnut

# The Plants we Eat

## What parts of plants are eaten?

Almost every part of plants is eaten, either by humans or by animals. Roots and leaves are often eaten, and some can be eaten by many animals as well as humans. Some root vegetables like carrots, beetroot and potatoes are often part of our meals. Others, like the root of the ginger plant, are less familiar to us. But it can be eaten fresh, or dried and turned to powder. In this form it is used to flavour many other foods. It has a warm and spicy flavour.

## What nuts and berries are used?

Many nuts are very popular as food, like the walnuts and peanuts below. Other nuts are used for animal food, or are turned into oil for cooking. The coffee bean is used to make the coffee we drink. The beans are inside the bright red berries, and these are dried and roasted before being ground to a powder. Many other plants are used for drinks: juice is *extracted* from fruit such as oranges and pears, or from root vegetables like carrots. Dried flowers, too, can be used in hot drinks.

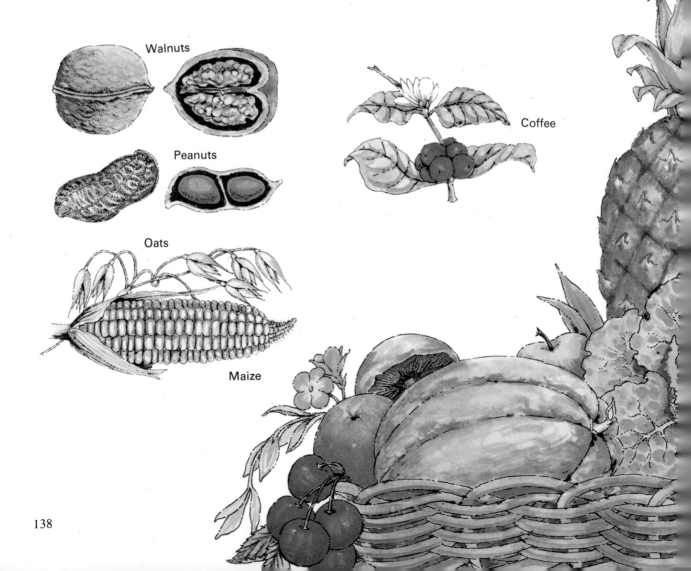

Walnuts

Peanuts

Oats

Maize

Coffee

## What stems and leaves do we eat?

Stems like that from the celery plant can be eaten raw, or cooked. The stem of the sugar cane is also used, but first the plant is chopped and pounded, and the sweet liquid sap is extracted. Sugar is used a lot in cooking.

We also eat a lot of leafy plants, like the lettuce in the picture below. The lettuce plant is almost all leaves: it has been bred like that by the growers. Other leaves that are eaten include cabbages, spinach, and herbs such as parsley and mint.

As well as these which people eat, many animals eat stems and leaves which we cannot. Their stomachs can *digest* a lot of material which humans cannot use at all.

Carrot

Beetroot

Ginger

Sugar cane

Celery

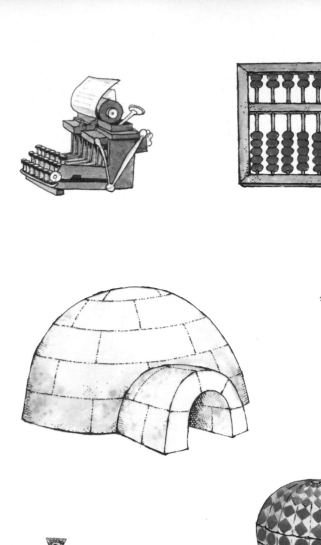

# HOW THINGS HAPPEN

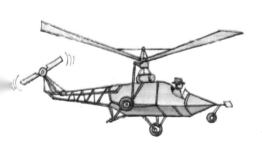

# All Kinds of Wheels

## Who first used wheels?

No one knows the exact answer to this question. Some people think the wheel may have been invented in ancient Mesopotamia. Mesopotamia was a land where the country of Iraq now lies. A stone slab has been found there with strange writing on it. Among the picture writing is a kind of sledge on four solid wheels. So people had thought of the wheel 4000 years before Christ was born.

## What were the early wheels like?

The earliest wheels we know about were made from three pieces of wood. You can see them in the picture above. They may have had circles of leather round the outside to help hold the wheels together. Wheels like this must have been very heavy and bumpy.

Some time around 2000 BC wheels with *spokes* were invented. This made the wheel much lighter and better. They could now be used on chariots.

It is interesting to think how much behind the times Britain was at this time. No one has found any traces of wheels with spokes in Britain before 500 BC. So ancient Egyptians were using chariots with spoked wheels 1500 years before wheels like this reached this country.

## What did people do before the wheel was invented?

Before the wheel, heavy loads had to be carried or dragged along the ground. Dragging loads was made easier by putting wooden rollers underneath. The ancient Egyptians used rollers to drag heavy stone blocks used in building the pyramids. It was probably using rollers like this that made someone think of the wheel.

It is even easier to lift weights by using two or more pulleys. The picture below shows how a rope passes over and round two wheels. It is called a *block and tackle* and is used to lift very heavy weights.

## Can wheels help to lift things?

Yes, indeed they can. A special wheel called the *pulley* was invented a long time ago. A rope is passed over a pulley wheel as in the picture above. Then a heavy weight can be pulled up more easily than by just trying to lift it straight off the ground.

## What are gear wheels?

Gear wheels are simple machines that change speed and help to do work. If the small wheel in the picture above turns once, the big wheel makes only half a turn. The small wheel has 9 teeth. These push the 18 teeth on the big wheel. The big wheel is turning at only half the speed of the small wheel. If we put an even bigger gear wheel with 36 teeth next to the left-hand wheel, it would go round at only a *quarter* the speed of the smallest wheel.

Gear wheels can also be used to make wheels go round faster. Look at the bicycle wheel below. Every time you make the pedal go right round once, the small gear wheel on the back wheel goes round several times. So does the whole back wheel. Many bicycles have several different gear wheels that help you to climb hills or move along speedily on the flat.

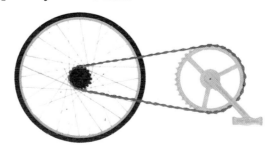

# Day and Night

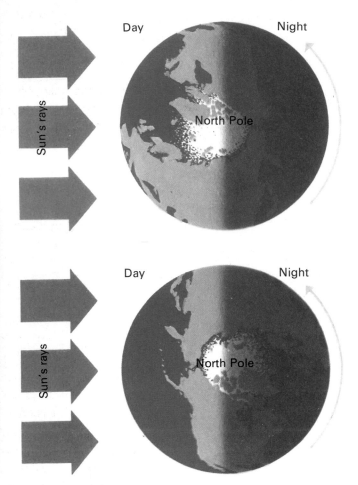

## Why do day and night last for different amounts of time?

Day and night happen because of the way in which the Earth turns as it circles the Sun. The Earth makes one complete turn every 24 hours. During that time, half the Earth's surface is always facing the Sun, and half of it is in darkness. So people in some lands have daytime, some have night, some see the Sun rising in the sky, while others watch it setting below the *horizon*.

If the Earth turned in just the same way all year, each day and night would last for exactly the same amount of time. But that does not happen. The Earth turns on a slant, and the *angle* of the slant is different throughout the year.

In our summertime, our part of the Earth slants towards the Sun. The Sun's rays shine longest on the parts of the Earth that are closest to it, so daylight lasts for longer in summer than in winter.

In our winter, our part of the Earth slants away from the Sun. We get less Sun-time in winter, and so the days are shorter. Night time happens when our part of the Earth is facing away from the Sun, and we have no light from it.

Above: In the top picture, the Sun's rays are shining on the bottom part of the Earth. It is daytime there. In the lower picture, the Earth has turned around. The other half of Earth has daylight instead.

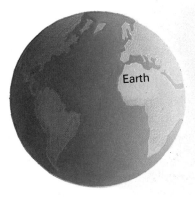

Right: You can see that the Sun's rays shine most on the part of Earth that faces it. On the other side, it is night. In between the light is less strong, making dawn and dusk.

## How many hours are there in a day?

There are 24 hours in one day, because that is the amount of time it takes for the Earth to turn around once. Our clocks, however, often tell the time in two sets of 12 hours . Eight o'clock in the morning, and eight o'clock at night, will look the same on this clock. When times are written down, we use *a.m.* for morning times, and *p.m.* for afternoon and night times.

## What is a 24-hour clock?

Some clocks show the time as one set of 24 hours. On a clock like this, 2 o'clock in the afternoon, or 2.00 p.m., is shown as 14.00 hours. This shows that it is 2 hours more than 12 o'clock, and no extra minutes.

Clocks like this are common now, because *digital* clocks and watches, which show the time in figures, are often sold. Many people who need to be absolutely sure of the time use a 24 hour clock. It is much harder to make mistakes about morning or afternoon times with this kind.

Day and night

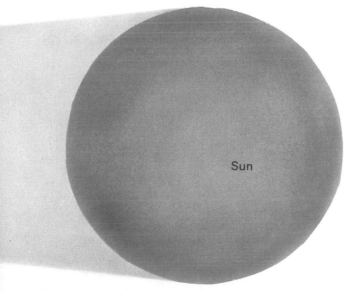

Sun

## Why do we sleep at night?

The very first people on Earth slept at night because they could not see to hunt in the dark, and it was safer for them to hide away from animals that *could* see! Sleeping at night and staying awake in the daytime sets up a pattern for our bodies. It is very hard to change the pattern around.

## Who sleeps in the daytime?

People who work at night, on shifts or in jobs that are done at night, need to sleep in the daytime. Babies sleep then too, because they need more sleep than adults. And half the world sleeps during your daytime – because while you have day, they have the night on the other side of the world.

# The Four Seasons

Winter

## What causes the different seasons?

In most of the world, there are four seasons during the year: spring, summer, autumn and winter. Summer generally has lots of sunshine, and the days are long; winter is cold and the days are shorter. In springtime the weather begins to get warm and the days lengthen, while in autumn it begins to get dark a little earlier, day by day.

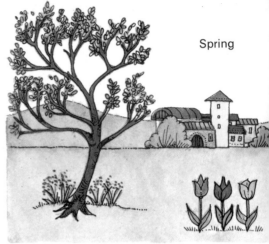

Spring

All these changes are caused by the different ways in which the Sun's rays strike the Earth during the year.

The Earth spins, like a top, day and night. It makes one complete turn every 24 hours. If it spun as if it were upright, the Sun's rays would always strike it in just the same way, and there would be no seasons at all.

But the Earth is tilted as it spins, and it travels around the Sun as it spins. When the tilt brings northern countries closer to the Sun, they have their summer and southern countries have their winter. As the *angle* of the tilt changes, so do the seasons.

Summer

## When do the seasons happen?

In northern countries, the hottest time is around the middle of the year. This is when the angle of the Earth's tilt brings the Sun's rays most directly to the land. The Sun is right overhead at noon, and daylight lasts longer than at other times of the year.

One day at this time is called the summer *solstice*; this is when there is more daylight than at any other time, and the Sun is as high in the sky as it can be. The winter solstice is just the opposite. It is the shortest day. When northern countries have their summer solstice, southern countries have their winter one instead.

Autumn

## Do all countries have seasons?

Because the seasons depend on where the countries are on Earth, not all places have four seasons. Even those which do have four seasons do not have just the same sort of weather during each of them. Countries close to the *equator*, the imaginary line that runs around the middle of the Earth, do not have seasons as we know them. It is generally hot and wet all year, and plants do not grow in the same way as they do in other parts of the world. This is because the Sun's rays strike the middle of the Earth in more or less the same way, all year.

The further north and south, away from the equator, the greater the difference between summer and winter. In the northernmost parts of the world daylight lasts so long in summer there is almost no night at all. In winter, the sun does not appear over the horizon for more than a few hours. And at the north and south poles, life is even more strange. Daylight lasts for six months at a time, and then night lasts for six months. If you lived at one of those places, you would have to go to bed in daylight in summer, and work all day in the dark in winter!

Picking apples

## Why is autumn the season of harvests?

In countries that have four seasons, the third of these is harvest time for most fruit, vegetables and grains. This is because plants in these countries grow in accordance with the time of year, and the weather that goes with that. It is too cold in winter for most seeds to sprout; most of them wait until spring to begin their growing. Then they use the long, warm days of summer to produce their flowers, fruit and new seeds. In nature, these would lie *dormant* in the wintertime, and grow the next spring. But we use autumn products for food, and so we harvest them when they are ready to pick.

Grain

Ploughed field

# Waves and Tides

## What cases waves?

Waves are caused by the wind. When wind blows on the surface of the water, it pushes some of the water down. This pushes another part of the water up into a wave.

## How big can waves be?

No one knows just how big ocean waves can be. But waves more than 20 metres high and 200 metres long have been seen by sailors.

## Does the water in waves move along?

No, it does not. The water in waves stays in the same place, even though it looks as though it is moving along. A piece of wood or a bird floating on the water is lifted up and down by the waves. It doesn't move

along. You can see what happens if you take a piece of rope, fasten one end and shake the other end up and down. Waves run along the rope, but the rope itself is only moving up and down.

## What causes tides?

As you soon find out when you are at the

The passing wave makes the bird go up and down.

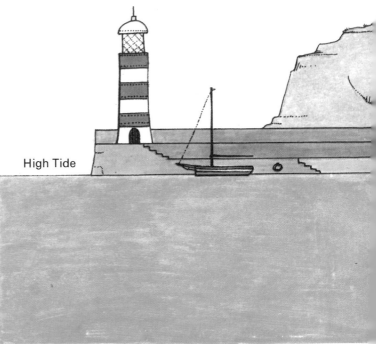

High Tide

148

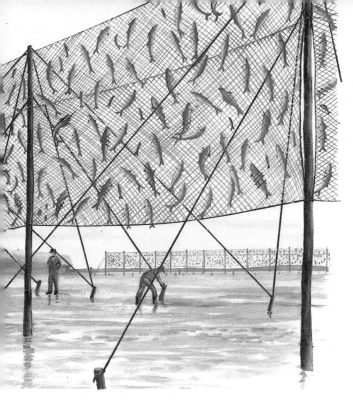

In the Bay of Fundy in Canada the tide rises as much as 15 metres. The fishermen use this great rise and fall to trap fish.

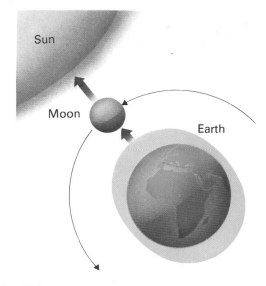

Spring Tides

## Are all tides the same?

seaside, the sea rises and falls twice every day. These rises and falls are called *tides*. They happen because the Moon and the Sun pull on the oceans as the Earth goes round and round. The Moon pulls harder than the Sun because it is very much closer.

No. Tides vary quite a lot. *Spring tides* happen when the rise and fall of the sea is large. *Neap tides* are not nearly so high.

During spring tides the Sun and Moon are in line with the Earth. The Sun and Moon pull together, so there are high tides. During neap tides the Sun and Moon are not in line, so they do not pull together. The tides are not so high. Spring and neap tides happen once every month.

Low Tide

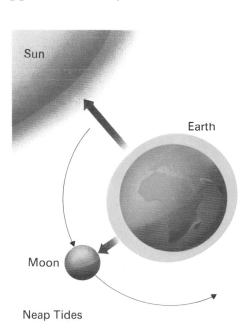

Neap Tides

# What Makes the Weather?

## What sorts of climate are there in the world?

The world's climates are divided into hot, warm, cool and cold. The hottest climate is close to the middle of the Earth, around the *equator*. The coldest climate is furthest away from the middle of the Earth, around the north and south poles. In between the equator and the poles, the climates are warm or cool.

Not all hot climates are the same. Some are called *tropical*. These places have a hot, wet summer and a winter that is dryer and cool. Other places with hot climates have winds that blow almost all the year, and there is very little rain at any time. These places are deserts.

In places that have a warm or a cool climate, the summer is warm and fairly dry, while the winter is cold and wet. But some places with warm climates have a rainy summer as well as a wet winter.

In a cold climate winter lasts much longer than summer. The winter weather is very cold, and it is often below freezing for months at a time.

Near the north and south poles it never gets above freezing at all. It is much too cold for people to live there.

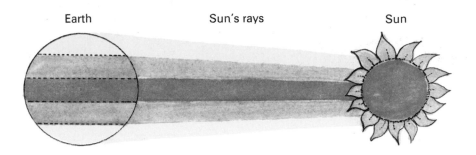

Earth · Sun's rays · Sun

## Why are climates so different?

Places that are close to the equator are hot because the Sun's rays come directly to the land. The Sun is always high in the sky and so the warmth lasts for a long time. Cold places only get the Sun's heat on a slant. The Sun is never very high in the sky.

## What is it like at the equator?

It is hot all year round in the lands along the equator. There are no seasons as we know them, with spring, summer, autumn and winter. Equator lands have lots of warm rain too, and plants produce their seeds and flowers all through the year.

## How do weather forecasters do their work?

Some changes in the weather can be worked out from watching the sky and the winds. Finding out about changes in the temperature and the amount of rain are other ways. Some sorts of cloud patterns bring rain or storms, and watching for these is a good way of knowing how the weather will change as well. But these only work for a few hours, or a few days, ahead. People need to know about weather for weeks, or even months, at a time. Modern weather forecasting has been developed to try to help.

The staff at weather stations get reports in from other stations all over the country. They also hear from countries close by, so they can work out if a storm there will mean a change for them too.

Radio reports arrive from ships at sea, and many countries have special aeroplane flights which take photographs of cloud patterns from high in the sky. Nowadays, satellite pictures are used as well. These pictures are taken from out in space. They give the cloud patterns over the whole Earth, and show the effect one climate might have on another.

All this information is put together by the weather forecasters. They can draw charts to show what today's weather is like, and compare those charts with the ones for the day before. Then they can work out what will happen in the future.

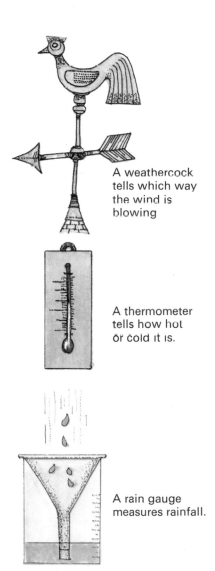

A weathercock tells which way the wind is blowing

A thermometer tells how hot or cold it is.

A rain gauge measures rainfall.

# Wind, Rain and Snow

### Why does it rain?

All the air around us has water in it. You can see water disappear when you watch a puddle on the road dry up when the sun shines.

When water dries like this, it turns into water *vapour* and mixes with the air. Water vapour in the air will, in the end, turn back into rain again. The amount of water vapour in the air helps decide what the weather will be like.

The air with water vapour at first is warm. But as it rises it cools, and turns into clouds. These sometimes become enormous, and pile up high above the Earth. As the air cools still further, the clouds cannot hold together any longer. Some of the water vapour in them turns back into rain, and falls back on to the ground.

This rain water collects in streams and rivers, and a lot of it flows back into the sea. There, when the sun shines, some water turns to vapour again, and the cycle begins once more.

### Why does rain turn to snow or sleet?

If the air around the clouds is too cold, the water in them will make ice crystals instead of rain. A snowflake is a bunch of ice crystals, which have joined together in a clump. Snowflakes only reach the ground as snow if it is cold enough. If the Earth is warm, the snow will melt into rain again.

Sleet is partly thawed snow. It falls if the air is not quite cold enough for snow, but too cold for ordinary rain.

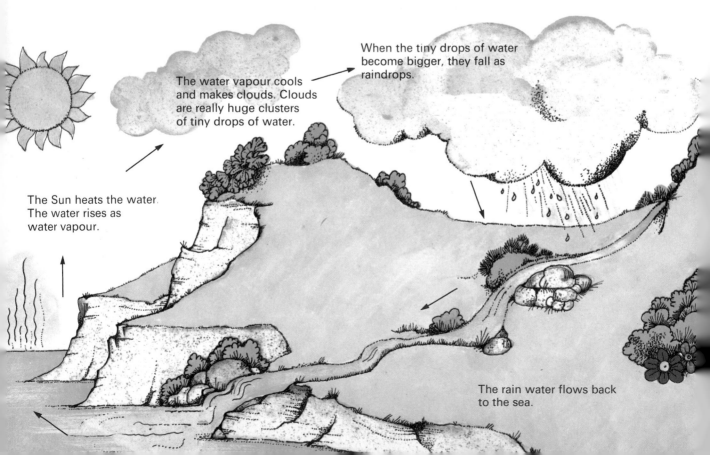

The water vapour cools and makes clouds. Clouds are really huge clusters of tiny drops of water.

When the tiny drops of water become bigger, they fall as raindrops.

The Sun heats the water. The water rises as water vapour.

The rain water flows back to the sea.

In high palces it is colder than in low places.

Force 1: Smoke drifts

## What makes the wind blow?

Wind is just moving air. You cannot see the air moving, but you can see what happens to things when the air pushes hard against them.

It is changes in the air temperature which cause the wind to blow, and the main cause of that is the Sun. This heats up the air, and the warm air rises. Cold air from nearby flows in to take the place of the warm, rising air. If this flows in fast and strong, we feel it as a breeze or a wind.

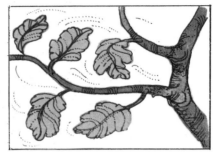
Force 2: Leaves rustle

## How can wind be measured?

The *force* of a wind – how hard it is blowing – can be measured. The pictures on this page show what different forces of wind can do. A force 1 wind is really just a gentle breeze, but a force 7 wind is a bad storm. It can move at enormous speeds and cause damage to anything that stands in its way.

Wind direction is shown by a *weather vane*. You can see weather vanes on the top of some buildings. A weather vane points in the direction from which a wind has come, and not the direction in which it is going. A south wind is blowing from the south towards the north.

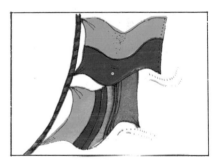
Force 3. Flags flap

Force 4: Twigs move

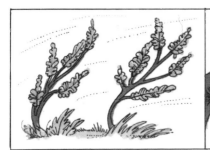
Force 5: Small trees sway

Force 6: Branches sway

Force 7: Trees move

153

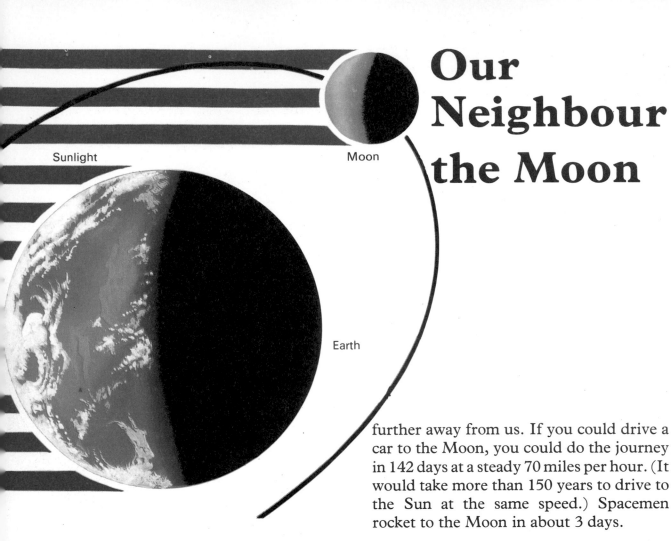

Sunlight

Moon

Earth

# Our Neighbour the Moon

further away from us. If you could drive a car to the Moon, you could do the journey in 142 days at a steady 70 miles per hour. (It would take more than 150 years to drive to the Sun at the same speed.) Spacemen rocket to the Moon in about 3 days.

## What makes the Moon shine?

When we look up at the sky on some clear nights, the Moon shines down like a great silver ball. On other nights it is only a thin slice. But the Moon does not really change its shape. It is always a round ball. The Moon seems to change its shape because we can only see the parts of it that are lit by the Sun. The Moon has no light of its own. The silver light we see is really sunlight bounced back to us from the Moon's surface.

## How far away is the Moon?

The Moon is easily our nearest neighbour in space. It is only about 390,000 kilometres away. The Sun is nearly 400 times

## Why does the Moon change shape?

The Moon goes right round the Earth every $29\frac{1}{2}$ days. It is our *satellite* and always

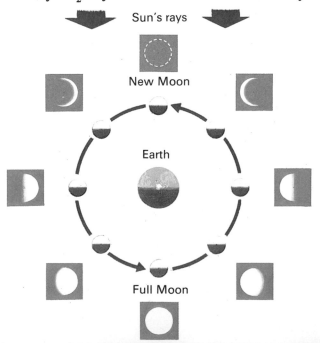

Sun's rays

New Moon

Earth

Full Moon

keeps its same face turned towards us. It is held in its near circle round the Earth by the pull of Earth's gravity. Most scientists think that our Earth and the moon were formed at the same time, about 4,500 million years ago.

You can see from the picture at the bottom of the opposite page why the Moon seems to change shape as it circles the Earth.

This picture shows the Moon as you would see it through a large telescope. People used to think that the big dark patches were seas. They gave them names like "Sea of Rains" and "Ocean of Storms". But now we know that there are no seas on the Moon. The dark patches are just dry, flat plains. The Moon is a dry, lifeless place. There is no rain, no wind, no clouds, no weather of any kind.

## How big is the Moon?

Can you guess how big the Moon is? Is it as big as the Sun? In fact, the Moon is not very big at all. It looks as big as the Sun because it is very much closer to us than the Sun.

## What is it like on the Moon?

The Moon is a dry, lifeless world. There is no air to breathe, no rain or snow, no wind, no clouds. The Sun blasts down its heat from a black sky. At midday the temperature in the Sun is a fiery 130° Centigrade – hot enough to boil water. During the Moon's night, the temperature on the surface drops quickly to a terrible —140° Centigrade. (The lowest temperature ever felt on Earth is —88° Centigrade.) You can see why spacemen have to wear special suits to protect them from the boiling heat and freezing cold. And the Moon is covered with strange holes called *craters*, like the one on the right. Some craters are 300 kilometres across.

The Moon is only about the size of Australia, as you can see in the drawing above. It is so small that it cannot hold an atmosphere around it, as the Earth does. So there is no air on the Moon. This is why spacemen who walk on the Moon have to take their own air with them.

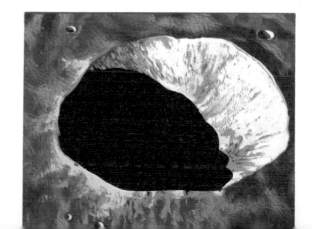

# All Kinds of Sound

### What makes sound?

The air is full of sounds – loud sounds, soft sounds, pleasant sounds and unpleasant sounds. The pictures on these pages show people and things making all kinds of sounds – the alarm clock's bell, the cat's quiet purr, the rattle, the drum, the police siren, bells, people talking and the music of a violin.

All these sounds are made by something moving in the air. Before our ears pick up a sound, something has to move quickly in the air to make the air *vibrate*. The vibrations travel through the air, and are called *sound waves*. We cannot see sound waves.

### Do sounds need air to travel through?

No, but they need something to travel through. They need air or water, a metal or something. If there were no air, we could stand in a busy street and hear nothing. There is no air on the Moon. If you were standing on the Moon and a gun was fired a few metres away, you would not hear it.

## What makes bangs from the skies?

Some aircraft fly faster than sound waves. As soon as a plane like *Concorde* reaches the speed of sound, the air ahead of it is disturbed. The disturbed air makes sound waves, and loud bangs are heard on the ground.

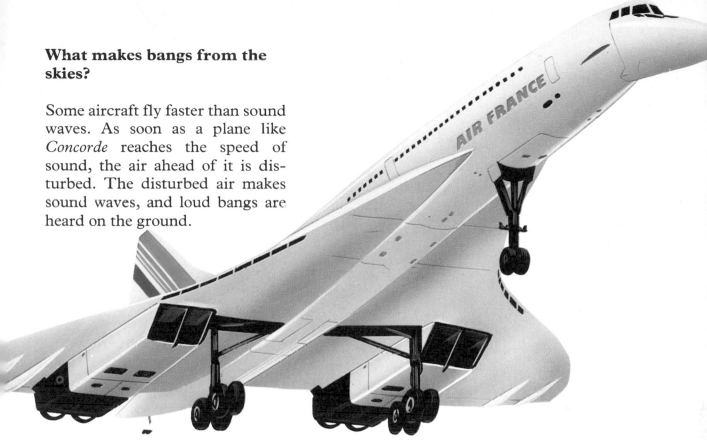

## Why does a bell clang?

Bells can be made of almost anything – clay, glass or even wood. But big bells are usually made of bronze – a mixture of copper and tin. When struck, they vibrate to make a musical note. The world's largest bell is in the Kremlin in Moscow. It weighs 196 tonnes, but it broke before it could be rung.

Gongs have been used in the East for hundreds of years. They are made of metal and struck with a soft-headed hammer. When struck they vibrate with a loud "boom".

## How far away is that thunderstorm?

Light travels about a million times faster than sound. You can tell this during a thunderstorm. The thunder and the lightning happen at the same time. But we see the lightning before the sound of thunder reaches our ears. If you hear the thunder 3 seconds after you see the lightning, the storm is about a kilometre away. If the delay is 5 seconds, the storm is about a mile away.

If you count the seconds between the lightning and the thunder and then do the same at the next flash, you can tell whether the storm is getting closer or not.

# Machines at Home

## When were the first machines made for homes?

A hundred years ago, almost no one had machines in their homes. Everything was done by hand, or just not done at all! Carpets were swept by hand instead of using vacuum cleaners. The only heat came from coal or wood fires, which had to be cleaned and re-made every day. Telephones and record players had not been invented. People wrote letters instead of telephoning, and they played the piano, sang and talked instead of listening to records or watching television.

The first telephones and record players did not look much like the ones we use today. They were very expensive too, so not many people could afford to own them. Some very strange-looking machines were invented in those early years. The one in the picture below was invented to make tea for people in the morning, but it looks very different from the sort people use now.

An early telephone, with a wind-up handle at the side.

## What other machines were made?

Sewing machines were invented in 1851 by a man called Isaac Singer. They were a great success. Electric kettles and irons came later, and gas and electric cookers were also introduced. All these made keeping house a lot easier – and cleaner – for everyone.

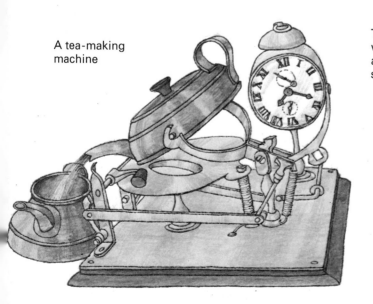

A tea-making machine

The first record players were called *gramophones*, and the speaker was shaped like a *funnel*.

Right: A Victorian bathroom.
**1** The bath, standing on legs. The water-heater, **2**, is connected to the shower fitting, **3**, above the bath. The basin, **4**, has the same decorations as the bath and the lavatory, **5**. The cistern, **6**, is also decorated.

Although this bathroom looks very old-fashioned to us, it was a very advanced addition to a Victorian household. Many houses did not have a bathroom at all. People washed in a tub in front of the kitchen fire, or in their bedroom. Most people did not bath often, because it was too hard to heat so much water all at once.

This carpet cleaner worked like an *accordian*, sucking in air from the carpet.

## What difference did the machines make to people's lives?

When the machines were used by lots of people, rather than just a few, they made an enormous difference. Many people in those days had servants to do the housework for them. Some of the servants did kitchen work, preparing food and washing dishes. Others did the cleaning around the house. If anyone wanted a bath, all the water had to be heated on the kitchen *range*. Then it had to be carried upstairs and tipped into a bath. All the clothes had to be washed by hand, and the water for this had to be heated in the same way. Clothes were made by hand as well. People used to say that all this work needed a lot of "elbow grease" – which just means a great deal of effort!

Washing machines, hot water *cisterns*, gas and electric stoves and fires, and sewing machines all changed people's lives. People were free to do other things with their time.

# PEOPLE AND PLACES

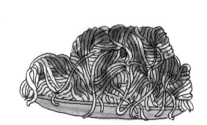

# Things we Build

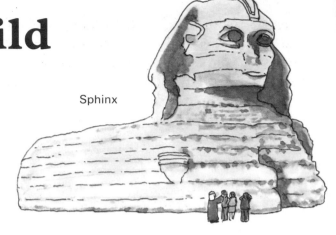
Sphinx

## Where is the Statue of Liberty?

The Statue of Liberty stands overlooking the harbour in New York City. It is a giant statue of a woman, 93 metres high including its pedestal. The woman represents the figure of Liberty, and holds a torch high in her right hand. The torch is lit up at night.

The Statue of Liberty was a gift to the USA from the people of France in 1884. It was carried in huge pieces by ship from France and put together when it reached the island in New York on which it stands. Inside the statue you can climb a long spiral staircase to the crown on the statue's head.

## What is the riddle of the Sphinx?

The great Sphinx at Giza, in Egypt, is a huge carving of a lion with the head of a woman. It was made over 4000 years ago in ancient Egypt. Sphinxes were an important part of ancient Egyptian myths. The ancient Greeks also told tales of sphinxes. In one famous story, the sphinx destroyed anyone who could not guess her riddle: "What is four-footed in the morning, two-footed at noon, and three-footed in the

Statue of Liberty

A mosque is a place of worship for people who follow the Islamic faith. Each day, a man called a *muezzin* stands in the high tower, calling the people to prayer. There are many beautiful mosques in the Middle East. They are decorated with tiny coloured tiles called mosaics and with fancy brickwork.

Mosque

evening?" Oedipus, a Greek hero, solved the riddle by replying: "Man, who in childhood crawls on hands and knees, in manhood walks upright, and in old age uses a stick."

## Who built this beautiful cathedral?

This cathedral looks like a fairy-tale building. But you can see it if you visit Moscow in Russia. It is the Cathedral of St Basil. Its beautiful bulb-shaped domes are decorated in many colours. Some of them are even painted gold. Tsar Ivan the Terrible ordered work to begin on the cathedral in 1554, but the building was not finally finished until 1679.

St Basil's Cathedral

Arch

## Why did people live in castles?

Hundreds of years ago during the Middle Ages people were ruled by many kings and princes who were often at war with one another. To protect themselves, these powerful men built great castles where they could be safe from enemies. Castles were usually built with thick walls and one carefully guarded entrance. Inside the castle were living quarters for the lord and his family, servants and soldiers.

Castle

A castle was like a little town. It was not just a home for the lord but also contained stables, workshops and a chapel. During a siege, peasants from the lord's lands often took refuge inside the castle.

# More Things we Build

### What is the Eiffel Tower and why was it built?

Towers are built for different reasons. Some towers are built mainly as radio and television masts – the Post Office tower in London was put up for this purpose. Other towers are built as *ornaments* – they look good.

The most famous tower in the world was built in 1889 as an ornament. It is the Eiffel Tower in Paris, named after a man called Eiffel who designed it for a big exhibition. The great steel tower was a wonder when it was built, and people who go to Paris still visit it. It is 300 metres high, and weighs over 7000 tons. On its top, the old tower now has television and radio masts.

You can climb to the top of the Eiffel Tower if you want to go up 1652 steps. Most people use the lifts.

### Why is the tower at Pisa famous?

Another, but much older, famous tower is in the Italian town of Pisa. It is called the Leaning Tower of Pisa because it leans so far over it looks as though it is about to fall down. The tower is the bell tower of Pisa's cathedral. It was begun in 1173, and it was only 10 metres high when it began to lean. But the builders, after a long time, finished the tower. It leans further and further over as time goes by despite attempts to stop it moving.

If you let out a piece of string with a weight at the end of it from the top of the tower, the weight would touch the ground about 5 metres away from the bottom of the tower. People come from all over the world to see the strange building.

There is a story that a great Italian called Galileo used the Leaning Tower of Pisa for an experiment. He dropped different weights from the top of the tower at the same time. They all hit the ground together. This showed that everything falls at the same speed, no matter how heavy or light it is.

164

## Are there different kinds of bridges?

People have been building bridges for thousands of years. Bridges are used to carry roads and railways over rivers and valleys.

The first bridge probably happened by chance. Perhaps a tree fell down and fell across a stream. Then people would chop trees down and place them across rivers and small valleys. Later, they may have supported the logs in the centre of the river with stones or other logs.

Another kind of simple bridge is the rope bridge. It is made from some long pieces of rope slung across the river. Rope bridges are still used in some parts of the world.

The bridge above is called an *arch bridge*. You can see there are two arches under which boats sail. The ancient Romans were very good builders of arch bridges. Some of their old bridges are still there.

There are lots of very big arch bridges all over the world. You may have seen pictures of Sydney harbour bridge in Australia. It is made of steel. Another big arch bridge is Waterloo bridge in London. It is made of concrete and has five wide arches.

The other main kind of bridge is the *suspension bridge*. These are hung by strong steel cables from tall towers at each end. The longest bridges in the world are suspension bridges. There is one in New York that has a span 1300 metres long.

## Where do people build lighthouses?

Lighthouses are often very difficult to build. They are built on rocks out at sea or on rocky cliffs or the entrances to ports. They are towers like the one above with lights on top. They help to guide sailors, especially at night.

The lights on early lighthouses were just fires burning in metal baskets. Today, lighthouses have powerful electric lamps and glass reflectors that bend the light into beams that can be seen for miles. Sailors can tell which lighthouse it is by the number of times the light flashes.

Many lighthouses also send out radio signals. Some sound a foghorn when it is foggy.

# How a House is Built

Architect

## How do people start building a house?

The building of a house begins with a person called an *architect*. Like the man in the top picture on the right, an architect is the person who plans out just what the house will look like. Every room is measured, the doors and windows marked in, the spaces for pipes and fittings worked out, and every detail is carefully checked. The architect has to be sure that everything fits together properly, and that the walls and floors are the right sort of strength for the jobs they do.

After the architect's plans are finished, many other people start on the work of building. The ground on which the house will stand may have to be cleared with a bulldozer. Then brick-layers will start to build the walls. Later, carpenters will make the wooden parts of the house and add them in where the plans show.

Bricklayer

## Are all houses made from bricks and wood?

Most houses in our part of the world are made with bricks, but some are made entirely of wood. Both these materials are useful because they are strong, last a long time, and keep out the wind and rain. Concrete buildings are also used, and flats are often made from concrete blocks. But bricks and blocks are sometimes covered with other materials after they have been used, so you cannot always see what the main material is in the building.

In some parts of the world other materials are more common in house-building. It often depends on just what is available nearby for the builders to use. Wood is very expensive in Italy, for example, and so it is not often used for houses.

Carpenter

166

## What happens after the outside layer has been finished?

The outside of a house is very important, but it is just the beginning of the job. The inside rooms have to have their walls built, the floors must be safe and firm, and the *plumbing* and *electricity* must be put in at the same time.

The plumbing in a house is the pipes and taps which carry the hot and cold water around to the rooms, like the kitchen and bathroom.

The electricity needs to be worked out too, so that there are enough *cables* to carry electric power to all the rooms. It is not just the lights that need electricity: the cooker, fridge, television and heaters all may need it too. If gas is used, this is added too, before the walls and floors are finished.

## When is the house finished?

Building a house may take months, or even years, to finish. It isn't much fun moving into a house which has no running water or lights! But when the builder has finished, and the architect is happy with all the work, the house can be used.

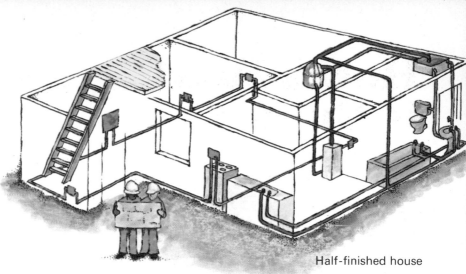

Half-finished house

Above: You can see the pipes for the plumbing in the half-finished house at the top of the page. Some of the things which need to be added are shown above – a heater, taps and a tank for hot water, and electric equipment like the switch, the bulb, and the ring on a cooker.

Below: The newly-finished house is now ready for its first family to move in.

# How Does it Grow?

### How do dates grow?

Dates grow on palm trees which can be as high as 27 metres. They grow only in hot countries such as Egypt and Iraq. Most dates are eaten in the countries in which they grow. In some desert places, dates are the only crop that will grow. The picture on the right shows a date palm.

### Where do oranges grow?

Oranges are *citrus* fruits, like lemons and grapefruits. Their juice is rich in sugar and other things that are good for us. Most of the world's oranges come from the United States, Brazil, Israel and Spain.

Sweet oranges are eaten raw. Bitter oranges are made into marmalade. The picture on the bottom right shows oranges growing in Israel.

### How does tea grow?

Tea grows mostly in India, Sri Lanka and China. Tea plants are green shrubs. The young leaves and shoots are first plucked when the plant is three or four years old. The leaves are then dried and become black. They are sent all over the world and finish up in the packets or tea-bags that we know.

The picture below shows women picking tea in Sri Lanka.

### How do peanuts grow?

Peanuts are also called *groundnuts*. They grow in hot lands on low shrubs. After the plant has flowered, thin shoots go down to the ground and bury their ends. The peanuts grow on the ends of these shoots underground.

When peanuts are crushed they give a lot of valuable oil. This oil is made into margarine, cooking fats and soap.

## How does rice grow?

Rice is one of the most important crops in the world. It is the main food of people all over Asia – more than half the people in the world. The young shoots are planted in flooded fields called *paddies*. Here they grow in a few centimetres of water until they are ready to be harvested. Young rice plants have long, narrow leaves. Clusters of flowers turn into the grains we eat. The picture above shows rice growing in paddy fields in China.

## How do grapes grow?

Most grapes are grown to be made into wine. They are also dried and turned into raisins, currants and sultanas. Grapes grow on bushes called *vines* and need long, dry summers to grow well. They are grown mostly in Italy, France and Spain. The picture below shows grapes being picked in a French vineyard.

## How does sugar grow?

There is sugar in lots of plants. But the plants that give us most of this sweet stuff are sugar cane and sugar beet.

Sugar cane only grows in hot countries. It is a giant grass from 4 to 6 metres high. When the tall canes are ripe they are cut and taken to a factory. There they are crushed to get the sugar juice. The picture below shows sugar cane.

# Making Sheep's Wool into Cloth

### How long has it been going on?

People have been making cloth for hundreds of years. The ancient Egyptians knew now to make fine linen from the flax plant. And the wool from sheep was used to make cloth before the time of Jesus.

### How much wool is there on a sheep?

Nearly all the woollen cloth we buy comes from the fleecy hair that covers the sheep's body. Some wool is made from goats' and camels' hair too. The best wool comes from Merino sheep. A really big Merino sheep's wooly coat will give enough yarn to make about 5 men's coats.

### How is wool yarn made?

First, the fleece is washed. This has to be done very carefully because sheep's wool holds a lot of grease and dirt. In modern factories the wool goes through several vats full of chemicals that clean the wool.

The wool is now a mass of short fibres, all tangled up. It is combed out to make it straighter. The combing used to be done by hand, as you can see in the picture. Nowadays it is done by great machines that comb the wool into a filmy sheet.

### What is spinning?

The wool is now ready to be spun into long lengths of yarn. The oldest way of doing this was by using a *spindle*. The people in the picture on the left are using spindles. They pull out the fluffy wool and feed it between their hands to the top-shaped spindle. The spindle is kept spinning so as to twist the yarn. The spun yarn is then wound onto the spindle. It is ready for weaving into cloth.

But using a spindle like this is not a very good way of spinning wool. Someone invented the spinning wheel, which did the job a little better. But spinning sheep's wool into long lengths of yarn was still very slow work. Today, huge machines spin the wool very quickly onto big reels. One machine can wind yarn onto 200 reels at the same time.

## How is yarn coloured?

It would be very dull if all woolen yarn was the colour of a sheep's coat. So, for more than 5000 years people have been using *dyes* to colour wool yarn and finished cloth. For a long time the only dyes they had came from plants and animals.

The women in the top picture are dipping the wool yarn into big tubs of dye. The coloured yarn is hung up in the sun to dry. Today, nearly all dyes are made from chemicals.

## How is woollen cloth made?

Wool yarn is made into cloth by *weaving*. Weaving yarn into cloth is done on a *loom*. One set of yarns is stretched over a frame. All these yarns go the same way. Then other yarns are threaded back and forth, under and over these first yarns. When all the yarns are tightened they make cloth. If different coloured yarns are used in a certain order, then coloured cloth is made. The two middle pictures on this page show people using looms that were used in days of old. Today, looms are big machines that can weave fine patterns very quickly.

When the cloth comes from the loom, it can be made into woollen coats and suits by the tailor.

# The Clothes of Different Countries

## Why do people in different countries wear different clothes?

The people in the pictures on this page all live in very hot countries. It is often much hotter where they live, than it ever becomes here. Sometimes the nights are cold, but the daytime Sun is so fierce it would make you sick unless you were used to it. You can see the sorts of clothes they wear for their countries' *climates*. Although their countries are not close together, their clothes look the same. They are all loose and long, and made from thin, light material. Desert Arabs wear clothes like these as well. When our country is sunny, we are used to wearing short clothes, or even just a bathing suit. But these people need to cover their skin from the Sun. They often wear something on their heads, too. This helps to protect their heads from the heat.

Nigerians

## What about cold lands?

People who live in cold countries need to dress for the weather as well. Their clothes are thick and warm, and people often wear lots of different *layers* of clothes to help keep the heat in next to their bodies. It is only when people live in countries that are not very hot or very cold, that they can choose to wear what they like.

An Indian woman

A Burmese man

Right: The clothes these people wear are good for where they live. Can you think of other lands where people wear clothes like these?

Moroccans

Dutch

Austrian

Spanish

## What is a national costume?

Most countries have a national costume, and the people in the pictures above are all wearing their own ones. A national costume is not worn every day, although many years ago lots of people in that country probably wore clothes that looked like it. But now such costumes are worn on special holidays, and at parties and festivals. The costumes show something from the country's history. They show what the people there used to do, and how they used to live. Wearing a national costume helps people to show they are proud to live where they do, and be part of their own land.

## Why are clothes important?

We all need to wear clothes, because our bodies could not keep warm without them. But we do not need to wear all the different clothes we choose – many of them do not just keep us warm. Some people like to wear clothes that are fashionable. Others like to wear clothes that show they belong to a group of people. Have you ever belonged to a group that had special clothes to wear? Clothes like that are called a *uniform*. Sometimes a special colour, or one bit of clothing, makes a uniform for people. Do you wear a uniform? What clothes do you like wearing best of all?

## How is a *sari* put on?

Indian women wear a special dress called a *sari*. These pictures show how it is put on. First, the material is tucked into her underskirt. Then the material is folded into *pleats* around her waist. The loose end of the material is folded over her shoulder. Now the sari is ready to wear.

# Special Clothes for Different Jobs

## Why do people wear special clothes when they do some jobs of work?

Some of the time, the clothes that people wear depends on the work they do. There are some jobs that need a set of tools to do them properly. A plumber needs to have his tools with him to clean out pipes and sinks, and a baker needs pots and pans and a good oven.

But other people need to wear special clothes. Some of these clothes are shown in the pictures on this page. Look at the things the people wear on their heads. The miner needs to protect his head from falling rock, and the fisherman and the trapper both need to keep their heads warm and dry. Why does the astronaut wear a helmet?

## How does special clothing help?

An astronaut is helped by the suit he wears. It keeps his body at the right temperature, and stops it being hurt. The suit is warm, but light to wear. A diver's suit does the same sort of job, but it is made from rubber. The rubber stops the water from making the diver cold and wet. The trapper needs to protect his body from cold weather.

Fisherman

Diver

Miner

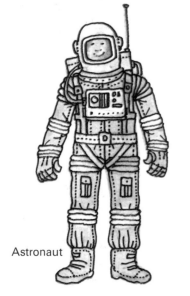

Astronaut

Trapper

Above: all these clothes are made to protect the people who wear them. *Protective* clothing is very important for many jobs, and ordinary people also wear some sorts of protective clothes. Trousers protect your legs from scratches and knocks. Boots protect your feet when you walk.

## What is a uniform?

People who are members of a group often wear a uniform to show they belong to the group. Some uniforms began as protective clothing, but are now worn to show who the person is that wears the clothes. All the people on this page are wearing uniforms. Can you work out which bits of their clothes are needed for their jobs? Which bits do you think are just for decoration?

Nurse          Soldier          Cook

**Some different police uniforms**

# People on the Move

## Who began the railways?

In 1804 Richard Trevithick built the first steam engine to run on a tramway at an ironworks in South Wales. But the first real engine was built by George Stephenson. Stephenson's engine won a prize offered by the new Liverpool and Manchester Railway in 1829. It was called the *Rocket*. Stephenson's father was a miner, born near Newcastle. The young George could neither read nor write until he was 18. But his locomotives became famous all over the world. For over 100 years engines were driven by steam. Today these engines have been replaced by powerful diesels in most parts of the world.

## How old is ballooning?

Today ballooning has become a popular sport. Every year there are balloon rallies and people try to break ballooning records. But the beginnings of ballooning go back to the 1700s. In 1783 two French brothers, Jacques and Etienne Montgolfier, built the first hot-air balloon. It was just a big bag with a hole at the bottom. A fire burned under the opening to keep the bag filled with hot air. As hot air rises, the balloon was lifted up above the heads of the amazed people who watched.

Glider

Balloon

Van

Caravan

Lorry

Travel by oxcart is one of the oldest kinds of transport. Oxcarts are still used in many parts of the world.

## How fast can we travel?

Until about 150 years ago people could not travel faster than a horse could take them. Then, in the 1830s people began to travel by the new railways. Railway routes began to spread all over the world and travel became easier and faster.

Today, jet planes like *Concorde* can cruise at speeds faster than 2000 kilometres an hour. They can cross the Atlantic in three hours. It would take relays of horses about 10 days to cover the same distance.

## Is the sky the limit to the speed at which we can travel?

Jet planes are not the fastest kind of transport. When spacemen are shot off the Earth by huge rockets, they travel at breathtaking speeds. To get away from the pull of mother Earth they have to travel at more than 11 kilometres a second – more than 40,000 kilometres an hour. If *Concorde* could travel at that speed it could fly from London to New York in about 8 minutes! And some day people will travel much, much faster than that.

Helicopter

Aircraft

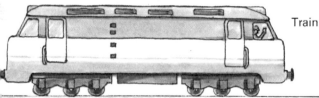

Train

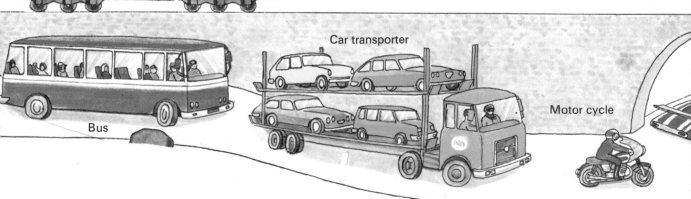

Bus

Car transporter

Motor cycle

# Where People Live

Camel

Arabs

## Can people live anywhere?

The animals in the pictures on this page live in just one sort of place. Seals like very cold places close to the sea. Camels like living in the desert. They eat the plants that grow there. What do you think would happen if a camel and a seal changed places? Could a seal live in the dry desert? Could a camel eat fish? The only animal that can live in many different places is the human.

Seal

Eskimo

## What do people need?

People need air, food and water to stay alive. They can find these things almost anywhere in the world. If you were not used to living in the desert, you would probably die there. But the Arabs in the picture above know just how to make their lives comfortable in the dry sandy land. They wear the right sort of clothes, and they know where to find food and water.

The Eskimo in the picture below has found how to live in the frozen north. Eskimos wear thick furs against the cold. They hunt for their food amongst the ice.

## Is there anywhere people cannot live?

There are places people cannot live on Earth. High mountains do not have enough air for people to breathe. Some land has no food on it at all. Other places have no fresh water. But as long as there is air and just a little food and water, humans can find a way to live their lives. They can make shelters, friends, and a life for themselves.

Right: Life in the high mountains in Europe means lots of walking up and down the steep slopes. The houses' roofs are weighed down with stones, to stop winter snow moving the tiles away.

### How do people learn to live in new and different lands?

It is hard to learn a new way of life, and it is especially hard to do that if the new place is not like your old one. If the food, weather and land are very strange for you, it will take many years to settle down. You will have to learn new skills, and you will have to give up some of your ideas for new ones. This is called *adapting*.

### Why do people move to other places?

People sometimes have to leave their home lands, and sometimes they choose to do so. A hundred years ago some people went to live in Africa. The picture below shows African jungle. Explorers from Europe went there to find out what it was like. Life in Africa was very different for them, and many found the country too hard for them. But the Africans knew how to live there.

Hippopotamus

Nomads

# Different Kinds of Homes

### Why do some homes move?

Many of us live in houses or flats. We stay in one place until we decide to move to a different house or a new area. But that may not be for several or even many years. In some parts of the world, people are on the move all the time. Herdsmen in Africa move about looking for grass for their animals. During the dry season, people are often forced to move to where there is water. People who move around regularly are called nomads.

Many tribes of nomads live in North Africa and the Middle East. Their homes are tents which they can put up and take down easily when it is time to move on. Tents have been homes for thousands of years.

A farm in Europe usually has a farmhouse for the farmer and his family and a barn for the animals.

One kind of African farm has many huts. Some huts are bedrooms and storerooms. Others are for the farm animals.

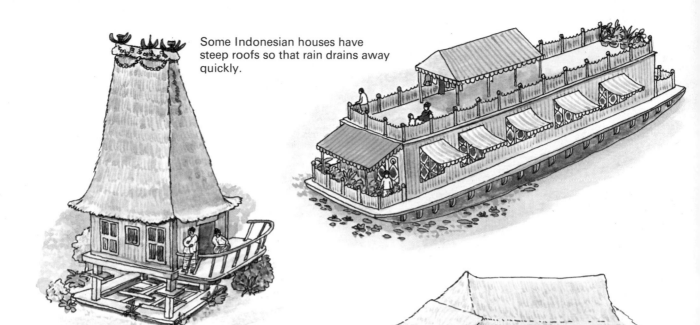

Some Indonesian houses have steep roofs so that rain drains away quickly.

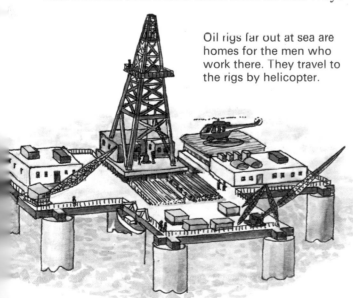

A house on stilts keeps out water along rivers and marshes in wet countries.

## What is wattle and daub?

Many tribal huts have walls made of wattle and daub. Wattle is the inside of the wall. It is made by "weaving" branches in the same way that cloth is woven. Daub is a mixture of clay and animal dung that is plastered over the wattle to make it weatherproof. Wattle and daub walls were used in houses in Britain and northern Europe for hundreds of years. Today the Masai tribe in East Africa still build their huts in this way.

Oil rigs far out at sea are homes for the men who work there. They travel to the rigs by helicopter.

## Can boats be homes?

Many people enjoy boats for holidays. But to others, boats are homes. Barges still carry cargoes on some rivers and canals, and in ports. Some of these are also used as homes by their owners.

Other people live in houseboats on rivers or in harbours. These homes often have heat, electricity and running water just like a house on land. Many houseboats are built in two storeys, with bedrooms upstairs. Often they have a sun deck outside, instead of a patio or porch.

Ships at sea are homes for their crews for large parts of the year. On a luxury liner, the crew have their own cabins, dining room and sometimes even a cinema.

A chalet in Switzerland has a gently sloping roof. When winter comes, the snow lies in a thick layer on the roof and helps to keep the chalet warm by keeping the cold air out.

## Which homes are biggest?

The biggest homes are palaces built by kings. One famous palace is at Versailles, in France. It was built by King Louis XIV in the 1600s. Versailles is large enough to house 10,000 people. It has huge gardens. In the time of Louis XIV, the flowers were changed twice a day! But Versailles was not just a home for the king. All his servants, courtiers and ministers lived there too. It was really like a small city.

## How do we keep houses warm?

Some people heat houses with log or coal fires. Others have electric fires or central heating. Water or air heated by a boiler is pumped to rooms all over the house. One kind of Dutch farmhouse has a very special kind of heating. The farmer and his family live in the front of the house. The cows live in a big room at the back. The heat from the animals' bodies keeps the farmer's rooms warm.

These Dutch houses stand on a canal in Amsterdam. Like many old Dutch buildings, they have stepped roofs.

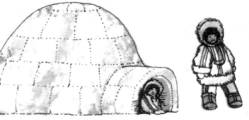

Some Eskimoes still build homes out of blocks of frozen snow. These homes are called igloos. They are warm and cosy inside and will not melt even if a fire is built on the foor of the igloo.

In cities, some homes are big blocks of flats. They are homes for many families. Other people live in big houses. Still others have houses of their own. Because there is not much space, people in cities have to live close together.

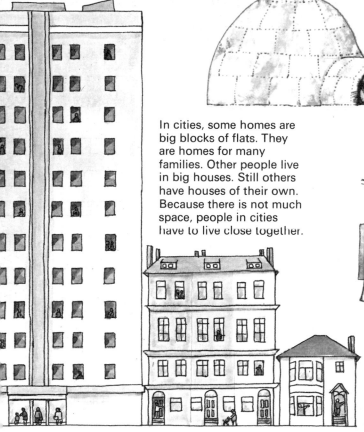

The houses in North Africa (above) have thick mud walls to keep out the heat.

Except for the windows and chimncy, this log house in Canada is made entirely of wood. Wood houses are common in countries where there are lots of forests.

Some American Indians build homes called tepees. They are made of skins stretched over a frame of wooden poles. These tribes were once nomads, and carried their tepees with them when they moved camp.

A gypsy caravan – another kind of moving home. These brightly coloured wagons were once a common sight on the roads in parts of Europe.

# What Flags Say

The Stars and Stripes

## How was the Union Jack made?

The Union Jack is a very unusual flag, quite unlike the flag of any other country. The making of the flag began in 1603 when England and Scotland had the same king for the first time. The king said that St George's cross of England should be joined with St Andrew's cross of Scotland.

Then, in 1801, St Patrick's cross of Ireland was joined to the other two. The result was the Union Jack as we know it.

When the Union Jack is flown, the wider white piece should be at the top, next to the flagpole.

The Union Jack is the flag of Great Britain. It also appears in the top corner of the flags of several other countries. Australia, New Zealand, Hong Kong and Fiji, all have the Union Jack on their flags.

British ships also fly flags with the Union Jack on them. Ships of the Royal Navy fly the White Ensign. This is St George's cross, with a small Union Jack in the top corner. British merchant ships fly the red ensign. It is all red, with a Union Jack in the top corner.

## Why does the American flag have 50 stars and 13 stripes?

Up until 1776, America was a British colony. Then the American people decided that they were not being treated fairly. They threw the British out of their country. There were then 13 states in the new America. So the American government decided to give their flag 13 white stars in a blue square and 13 red and white stripes. The flag became known as the Stars and Stripes.

As the United States of America grew, and more states joined the Union, the number of stars on the flag grew too. The number of stripes is still the same as in the first flag. But there are now 50 states and 50 white stars, as you can see in the picture on the left. The last two states to join the Union were Alaska and Hawaii, both of which joined in 1959.

The Union Jack

St George's cross

St Patrick's cross

St Andrew's cross

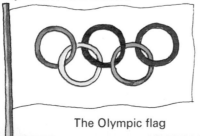

The United Nations flag

## Which flags do not belong to any one country?

There are several flags which are international – they don't belong to any one country. The flag of the United Nations is one. It shows a map of the globe, with two olive branches standing for peace.

Another international flag is that of the Olympic Games. Its five entwined rings stand for the five continents, and for friendship between them.

The Olympic flag

## Which other flags are international?

Flags used by sailors to send messages at sea are international – they can be understood by sailors of most countries. Each ship has a code book which tells sailors what certain groups of flags mean in their language. Signallers can also spell out words, since each letter of the alphabet has its own flag.

The most famous flag signal ever hoisted was the one ordered by Admiral Nelson before the Battle of Trafalgar. As the British fleet moved into battle, flags were run up in Nelson's ship which said to the whole fleet: "England expects that every man will do his duty".

Some signal flags hoisted alone have special meanings. The "P" flag hoisted alone means that a ship is about to sail. It is called the Blue Peter by sailors. The letter "V" means "I need help"; the letter "O" means "man overboard"; and "G" means "I want a pilot".

Flag signals were still used a lot between ships in convoy during the last war. Unlike radio, flag signals could not be picked up by the enemy.

185

# Big Ships and Little Boats

## How big are the biggest ships?

Until the 1960s, when air travel took over, the great passenger liners carried people across the oceans. The *Queen Mary* and *Queen Elizabeth* were two famous liners which made regular crossings of the Atlantic Ocean. At under 100,000 tonnes, they were the two largest passenger liners afloat. When it became cheaper and faster to cross the oceans by plane, both these ships were retired. The *Queen Elizabeth* was replaced by *Queen Elizabeth II*, a smaller ship that looked very different.

Today the biggest ships do not carry passengers. They are the tankers that carry huge cargoes of oil to countries all over the world. The biggest of these is nearly 500,000 tonnes, about five times the size of the great "Queens".

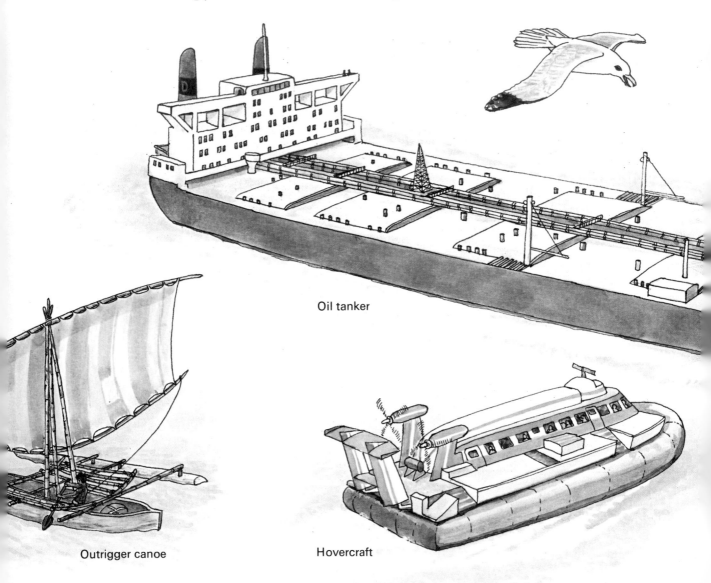

Oil tanker

Outrigger canoe

Hovercraft

## Can boats fly?

Some boats can skim over the surface of the
water as though they were flying. These
boats are called hovercraft. Hovercraft ride
along on a cushion of air without touching
the water. Air is pumped downwards
through nozzles around the edge of the hull
to raise the hovercraft. A skirt round the
bottom of the hovercraft keeps the air
under it to make the cushion.

The first hovercraft was launched in
1959 at Cowes in the Isle of Wight. Today
huge hovercraft carry passengers and cars
across the English Channel to France.
Hovercraft can also go over land. This
makes them good for exploring and as
rescue craft. They can reach the scene of
accidents quickly.

Hovercraft make good craft for navies,
too. Enemy submarines cannot hear their
engines or detect them with instruments
from under water.

Lighthouse

## What was the *Marie Celeste*?

In 1872 the ship *Marie Celeste* was found
floating between Portugal and the Azores.
Her sails were set, but all the people on
board were missing. The ship's one boat
and some instruments for navigating were
also gone. No one ever found any sign of the
crew or their instruments. Why they dis-
appeared is a mystery that has never been
solved.

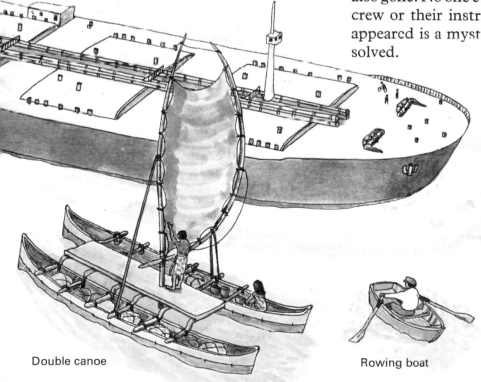

Double canoe

Rowing boat

## What are junks?

Junks are a common sight on the seas off China and South East Asia. They have four-sided sails stretched over many cross-pieces of wood. In Hong Kong many people live and work on their junks. Depending on its size, each junk may be a home for one or more families.

## How do you make a dugout canoe?

First, find a big log and chop a hole in it with an axe.

Next, burn out the hole to make it bigger.

Galleon

Clipper

Yacht

Chinese junk

## How do ships work for us?

Cargo ships and oil tankers are only two kinds of ships that work for us. Many other boats and ships are specially built for the jobs they do. Ferries carry passengers and often cars across short stretches of water. Trawlers are built for fishing. Tugs guide larger ships into harbours. Lightships are anchored near rocks or sandbanks to flash warnings to other ships. Lifeboats rescue people when ships are in trouble at sea. And icebreakers keep ports and rivers open in winter in cold countries.

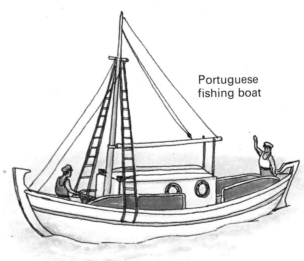

Portuguese fishing boat

Shape the ends of the log. Finally, smooth out the inside of the canoe and fix a seat to it.

## What is a trireme?

The ancient Greeks built great war-ships that were propelled by sails and oars. The biggest of these had three rows of oarsmen on each side of the ship, one row above the other. They were called *triremes* (*tri* means three). Ships with only two rows of oars on each side were called *biremes* (*bi* means two). Often, these ships had prows that were specially shaped for ramming enemy ships. They were sometimes decorated with fearsome faces to frighten enemies that saw them coming.

## When were the great days of sailing ships?

Ships and boats with sails have been built for thousands of years. The ancient Egyptians, Greeks and Romans all built ships called galleys that had sails and oars.

Later ships were designed with sails only. Shipbuilders built larger and larger ships with more and more sails. Men-o'-war carried heavy cannon. These ships were bulky and slow at sea.

By the 1800s ships had to travel long distances. They carried goods from colonies far away in Asia, Africa and Australia back to Europe. New ships began to appear that were sleek and fast. They were called clipper ships. With their sails unfurled, the clippers were a graceful sight as they ploughed through the waves. The British clipper *Sir Launcelot*, a famous tea clipper, was able to sail from China to England in 85 days. This was very fast in the days when the same journey could take four to six months. Another clipper, the *Cutty Sark*, carried wool from Australia to England. This famous ship can be seen today at Greenwich, in London.

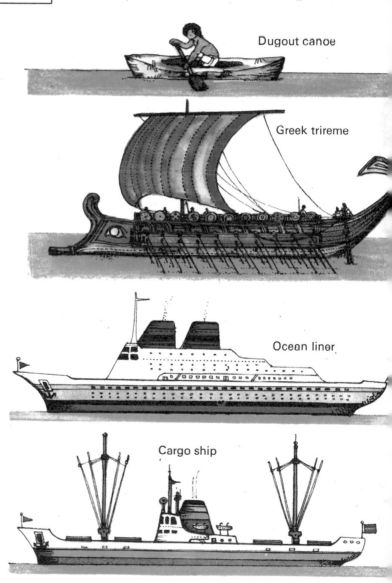

Dugout canoe

Greek trireme

Ocean liner

Cargo ship

# Inside a Ship

**What happens inside a ship?**

Many ships carry both cargo and passengers. The ship below is like that. You can find out what happens if you read the coloured panels.

The passengers sleep in roomy cabins and eat in their dining room. The crew sleep further down in the ship. They have their own dining room next to the kitchen. The kitchen in a ship is called the galley.

The chart room on the left is where the navigating officers work. They find out where the ship is at sea.

In the radio room the radio officer sends messages to shore stations and to other ships.

The long rod that turns the propeller is called the propeller shaft. The propeller turns in the water and pushes the ship along. Often there are two propellers, and two separate engines.

The engine turns the propeller shaft. Most ships today burn oil and use turbines. Many have diesel motors, rather like huge car engines. It is very important that the engine does not break down.

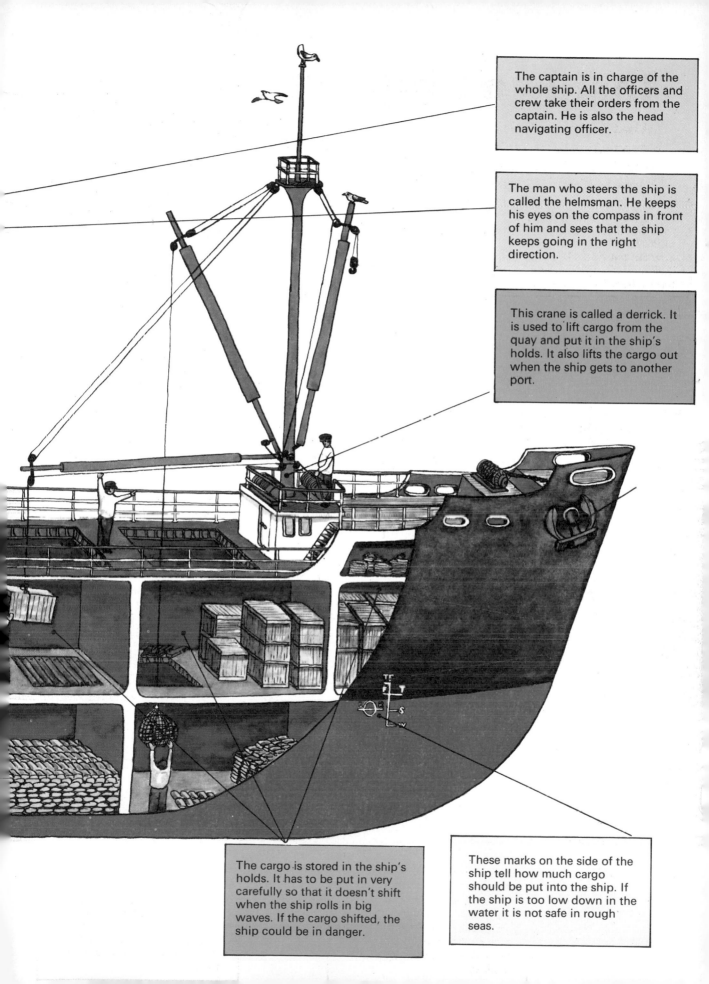

The captain is in charge of the whole ship. All the officers and crew take their orders from the captain. He is also the head navigating officer.

The man who steers the ship is called the helmsman. He keeps his eyes on the compass in front of him and sees that the ship keeps going in the right direction.

This crane is called a derrick. It is used to lift cargo from the quay and put it in the ship's holds. It also lifts the cargo out when the ship gets to another port.

The cargo is stored in the ship's holds. It has to be put in very carefully so that it doesn't shift when the ship rolls in big waves. If the cargo shifted, the ship could be in danger.

These marks on the side of the ship tell how much cargo should be put into the ship. If the ship is too low down in the water it is not safe in rough seas.

# The Food we Eat

## What sorts of food are there? Which ones are good for you?

Our food can be divided into different groups. They are all important, because they all give different sorts of nourishment to our bodies. It is important to eat many different foods, not just one sort. This helps people to stay healthy, and it is also good for their *appetites*. If you ate the same thing at every meal you would soon get very bored!

Fruit and vegetables are one group of foods. These are good for you when they are raw, as well as when they have been cooked. Milk and things made from milk are another group; cheese, yoghurt and butter are all made from milk. Eggs are a good food, because they give us *protein* and *vitamins*. Many people also like eating *poultry*, like chicken.

Grains like wheat, rice and corn are the most popular food. They are eaten in many different ways: as flour in bread and cakes, and in cereals for breakfast.

Milk

Cheese

Yoghurt

Butter

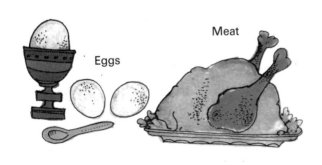

Eggs

Meat

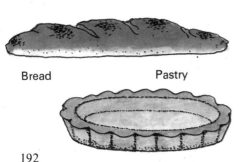

Bread

Pastry

Buns

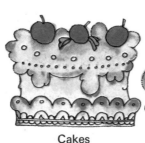

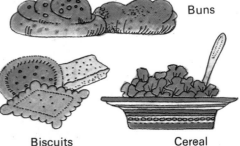

Cakes

Biscuits

Cereal

Soup
Salad
Jam
Pies
Vegetables
Fruit salad

## How many meals should we eat?
## What sort of meals are best for you?

Most people in the rich countries of the world eat three meals a day. A lot of those people also eat snacks at other times. There are lots of people, however, who are lucky if they get just one meal a day. Doctors think that the best kind of meal to eat is a small one, with not too much sweet food in it, and as much raw vegetables and fruit as possible. They think it is better to eat more food at the start of the day than at the end of it. But most of us have our main meal in the evening, or in the middle of the day.

A main meal often starts with a dish like soup. The next part, or *course*, is often a meat dish with vegetables or salad. The end of the meal is usually something sweet, like a pudding, but a plate of fresh fuit is better for you.

## Do people like the same foods?

The sorts of food people like to eat are often different from country to country. Many kinds of food began in a particular country, and have become a sort of national dish.

Pasta dishes, like spaghetti, were first cooked in Italy. Now people all over the world enjoy them. Chinese and Japanese people like rice with their food at all their meals. Some countries, like India, have become famous for their spicy foods. Every country has a style of food and cooking, all its own.

## Could you eat these things?

Snails have been eaten for hundreds of years – the Romans enjoyed them, and French people still do. Frog's legs are also very popular in France. Octopus and snakes, as well, are thought to be delicious by many people. It all depends on where you live, and what you think of as food.

Snails

Octopus     Snakes

Frogs' legs

# On the Farm

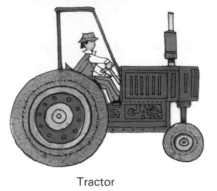

Tractor

## Why are machines used on farms?

The farms in rich countries today all use many different machines. The farmers need machines to produce good crops quickly. They could not grow so much food on their land without machines to do a lot of the work.

## What are the main farm machines?

The most important farm machine in the world is the *tractor*. Tractors pull a huge number of different field and crop *attachments*, like the ones you can see in the pictures on the opposite page. Tractors are good on steep ground as well as flat, and they are sturdy and reliable.

*Dairy* farmers in many countries use milking machines to get milk from their herds of cows. One person milking by hand can do only one cow at a time. But one person can milk up to 40 cows at once if they use a milking machine.

The same sort of speed is true with electric *shearing*, too. Shearing the wool with hand clippers is slow and hard, but using electric shears on the sheep makes the job much easier.

If you are in the countryside when wheat and corn are being harvested, you will probably see *combine harvesters* at work. These machines have made a great difference to farmers. The machine cuts the wheat, separates the grains from the stalks, and gets the stalks ready for *baling*. Before the machine was invented, these things had to be done separately. It all took a long time. Now a big field can be finished in just one day.

Milking machine

Electric shears

Combine harvester

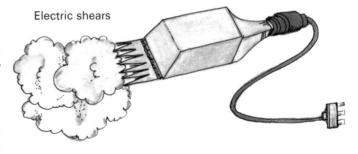

## Are farm machines expensive?

A lot of farm machines cost a great deal of money, so farmers have to make sure the ones they buy are worthwhile. They have to remember that the machines need to be looked after by *mechanics*, and that the fuel to make them work costs money as well. Some farmers cannot afford to buy lots of expensive machines. Instead, a group of farmers might buy a machine to share among themselves. Some farm machines, like combine harvesters, can be hired by a farmer when he needs to use them. Hiring a machine is cheaper than buying it, so the farmer saves money.

A tractor pulls a plough

A tractor pulls a seeder

## What other work can farm machines do?

Farm machines are made to do almost all the work you can think of. There are machines to weigh, feed and check the progress of farm animals. Other machines add water to land when it's needed, and harvest all sorts of crops – from wheat to fruit – and only need people to look after the engines.

## What machines are used all year?

You can see in the pictures above, and in the one below, that the tractor is used all year round on a farm. First of all the land is prepared to make it ready for planting. The tractor pulls a plough through the soil to make it soft and even. Then the seeder is pulled along, and the seeds drop into place. Last of all, the grains and stalks are harvested when the wheat is ripe.

A combine harvester cuts the corn, and a tractor and cart collects the straw.

# People at Work

## What sorts of jobs do people do?

There are hundreds of different jobs for people to do in the world. Some of them take just a short time to learn. Others take years of training. Some jobs have to be done where other people live, but others can be done thousands of miles from a town or city.

A lot of people are paid for their work, but many people work without earning money at all. What sort of work you do depends a lot on who you are, and where you live. It depends, as well, on what you are able to learn.

What sort of job would you like to do? What will you have to learn about first, to do the job properly?

These pictures show different sorts of jobs in a *restaurant*. The *chef*, above, works in the kitchen. There the food is prepared and cooked for the people who come to eat. The *waiter* takes the food to the people at the tables. He serves the people with food and drink. The people at the table are doing their job too! If they did not come to eat the food, the restaurant could not stay open.

## Why do people work?

Most people work because they have to. Their lives would not be possible without doing a job of some kind. People have to have a place to live, food to eat, and clothes to wear. In most countries in the world, these things have to be bought with money. So people need to earn money by doing a job.

## Who can work?

Many countries have laws that say who can work. Children are often not allowed to work for money, until they are old enough. Sometimes women are not allowed to do certain jobs, or work at all.

Below: A gondolier in Venice rows his gondola through the canals.

## Are all jobs hard to do?

Some jobs take a long time to learn. This is usually because the job is a complicated one, and you have to be trained to do it properly. The *gondolier* in the picture above had to learn his job. It looks quite easy, but it is hard to steer a gondola around narrow canals that are crowded with other boats.

## Which jobs are easy?

If a job is easy to do it may be a bit boring as well. Lots of people find boring jobs hard, because they would rather do something interesting. So perhaps no job is really easy. Most people find their jobs easy sometimes, and hard at other times. It is more important to do a job that you like and find interesting, than to do an easy one.

Left: This man is collecting rubber from rubber trees in Malaysia.

Right: Ballet dancers have to train for many years to do their job.

197

# Things People Make

## Why do people make such a lot of different things?

Many countries are famous for the things they make. Some of these are special to the country – they are not made anywhere else in the world. Such things are called *traditional* to a country. They are part of that country's history, and way of life. They have developed over hundreds of years to look the way they do now. So, because people in different countries live in different ways, the things they make are different too.

Right: This doll is made in Russia. It is made of wood, and it unscrews. Inside the doll is another, smaller doll. That one unscrews as well. Inside it is another, even smaller doll. Sometimes the dolls are made so that the big one has 8 or 10 dolls inside it.

## Who makes the traditional things?

In many countries people are trained to make their special *crafts*. Some skills are handed down from parents to children. Some skills are taught to people by others in their village or community, or by the government.

## Who buys the craft work?

Many things are made for visitors to the country. The visitors buy the things to keep as *souvenirs* of their holiday. Other things are made to be sold to other countries. But some of the traditional things are still made for home use.

This woman lives in Peru. She is weaving mats by hand, in the way people in Peru have done for centuries.

## What patterns are used?

People often use a *pattern* that is the same as the one their village or group has always used for making things. The woman in the picture on the left is weaving a mat. The patterns she is using have been the same for many hundreds of years. They show the animals of the countryside around her home. The tools she is using are also the traditional ones that have been used in the past. It takes a long time to weave by hand.

Glass-making in Italy is often done in the traditional way. This man is blowing melted glass through a pipe. He will turn it into a beautiful jug.

In Mexico, many people make bright paper flowers to sell. They also make traditional jewellery from silver, and use pretty stones to decorate it.

## Why do people like traditional crafts?

Many people like traditional work because it is so different from other sorts. Things made in a factory often all look the same. But something made in the old way is very special It shows how clever people can be with their hands.

## Are there any new traditions?

Traditions begin in a group of people when they need to have something just right for their way of life. This means that new traditions begin all the time, as life changes. New crafts show better ways of doing things, and take over from the old ways. Some modern things today might become traditions for the future.

Right: Carpet-weaving in Turkey is a traditional craft. The carpets are woven on enormous *looms,* and bright colours are used to make a pattern. Many people in other countries buy carpets like these. They last for a long time.

# At Work in a Factory

Above: The manager of this toy car factory dictates a letter to his secretary.

### What is an assembly line?

Many things, such as cars, are made on an assembly line. This means that the product moves from worker to worker. Each worker has a different job to do. For example, in a car factory the car begins as a steel frame

The factory workers make the toy cars. Each worker has a special job to do.

A worker takes the finished cars to the packers.

called a *chassis*. As it moves along the assembly line, each worker or group of workers adds something to it – the engine, gears, electrical equipment and so on. The car rolls off the end of the assembly line completely finished and ready to be shipped to a car dealer.

This kind of assembly line was invented by Henry Ford as a way of making his Ford cars in the early 1900s. It made cars cheaper to produce, and so cheaper for people to buy. Today, parts of some car assembly lines are "manned" by robots. Many other products are made entirely by machine.

### What does the factory manager do?

The manager must make sure that everything runs smoothly in the factory. He or she is in charge of all the workers, from the sales people who sell what the factory makes to the nurse in the medical room who looks after sick or injured workers. The heads of all the factory departments tell the manager how work in each department is going. If there are any problems it is the manager's job to sort them out. In turn, the manager reports to the directors or owners of the company.

Office workers answer the telephone, keep the files and type letters.

## The workers on the factory floor make and package a product. What do the workers in the factory office do?

The packers put the toy cars into boxes. Packing in many factories is done by machine.

Before any products can be made, the factory must buy the materials it needs to make them. When the product is finished, it must be shipped to the people who will sell it. The office workers make sure that materials come in regularly. They help the finished products get to the right places. All the letters and files needed to keep the factory running smoothly are kept in the office. Office workers must also make sure that all the factory workers are looked after and paid their wages.

Keeping track of the factory accounts is also an office job. This work is done by accountants in an accounts office.

The boxes of cars are loaded into a van. The van will deliver them to the shops where they will be sold. Some may be stored in a warehouse.

1

2

# How a Town Grew

**What makes a town grow bigger and bigger?**

Long, long ago some people built a small village near a river. The river gave the people water and fish (1).

As time went by, more people came to the village. They built a bridge across the river. One family from the village grew rich. They built a big house (2).

The rich family built a factory where a farm had been. People came to work in the factory, and ships carried goods that the factory made. More houses were built and the village became a small town (3).

Then the railway came and the town grew more quickly. There were more factories, more bridges and still more houses. The big house was pulled down and a factory was built where it had been (4).

Many of the old houses were knocked down, and new tall flats were put up. This is how the town looks today (5).

4

3

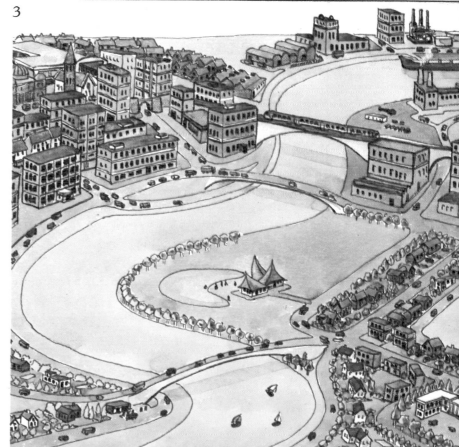

5

# How People Live Together

### What sort of place is best to live in?

The best sort of place to live depends on the people's lives. If you want to be a plumber, you need to live close to other people who will need to use the skills you have. You will have to be near people who have houses with taps and pipes and running water. If you are a farmer, you need land that is good for growing plants, and for feeding animals. In ancient times the most important thing was being able to grow or gather enough food to stay alive. Houses were built close to fields and grazing land. Later, people built their houses in groups. Being together made people feel safe against enemies. They could help each other in times of danger.

### What were the first villages like?

The first villages were very small, but in time they grew larger and had more families living in them. Some villages were built on the tops of hills, like those in the picture below. This was a good idea, because the people in the village could see what was happening in the valleys around them. It was also a good idea because the houses did not use up farm land. The people left their villages in the early morning and went to work on the land. Then, in the evening, they returned to their homes. The village was often surrounded by a high wall. The wall made the village a safer place. It was hard to attack a village with a strong wall.

## What is a community?

A *community* is a group of people who live together. They all depend on each other for help and support. Some of the people work at producing food or selling it, while other people do different jobs. The picture below shows an island community. What sorts of jobs do you think the people do? The bottom picture shows a village in Europe. Do you think the jobs there will be different?

## What do communities share?

The people who live together share lots of things. We share our hospitals, schools and shops with the people who live in the same place. We share the rules that say what we can and cannot do. The rules help us to get food, and homes, and work. If we did not have the rules, it would be hard to live in a community. When you play games with your friends you have rules to follow. What happens when someone breaks the rules?

# How Your Body Works

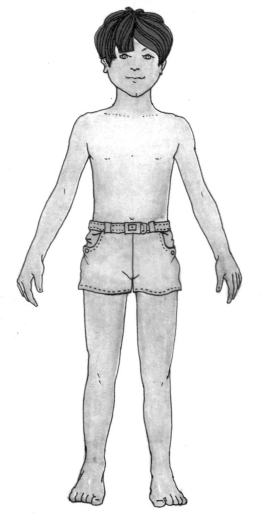

### Why do some people say our bodies are like machines?

Your body is like a machine in some ways. Like a machine, it is full of different parts that work together. It needs fuel, as a car needs petrol. The food we eat is fuel. And, like a machine, your body can break down if not looked after.

### Why do we need bones?

If you did not have a bony skeleton you would not be able to stand up. You would be a big blob of jelly! We have more than 200 bones in our bodies, all joined together by *joints*. The joints allow us to move.

Our bones do another important job. They guard the most important parts of our insides. The bony skull is a tough case to protect the brain. The bones of our chest – our *ribs* – make a strong cage for our heart and lungs.

### Why do we breathe?

When you run up a flight of stairs you get out of breath. You breathe more quickly, sucking in a lot of air. This is because your muscles have been working hard and have used up their oxygen. Oxygen is an invisible gas in the air we breathe. Without it our bodies cannot work.

We take air into our *lungs* by squeezing in our rib musles as in the left-hand picture. Our lungs stretch and fill with air. When we let our chest muscles relax, the lungs are squeezed and the used air is pushed out through our nose.

Our lungs sort out the useful oxygen from the air and send it in our blood to all parts of our bodies.

Breathing in

Breathing out

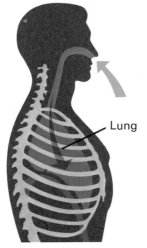
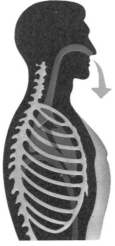

Lung

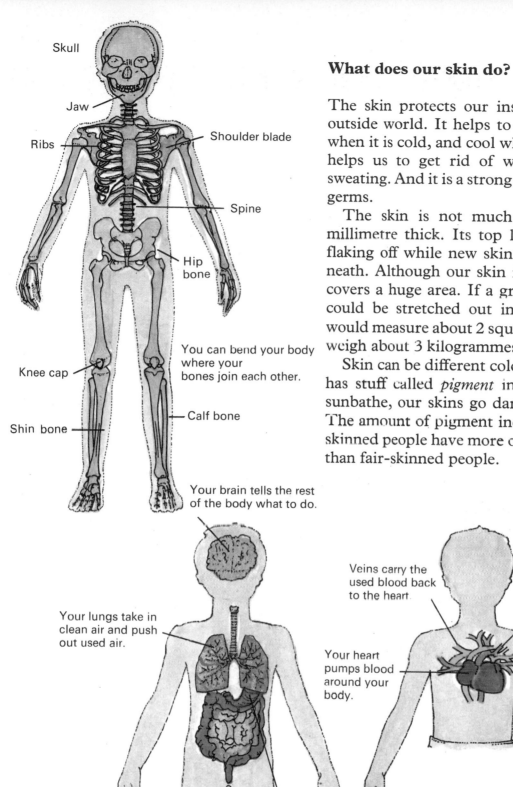

Skull

Jaw

Ribs

Shoulder blade

Spine

Hip bone

You can bend your body where your bones join each other.

Knee cap

Calf bone

Shin bone

## What does our skin do?

The skin protects our insides from the outside world. It helps to keep us warm when it is cold, and cool when it is hot. It helps us to get rid of waste water by sweating. And it is a strong barrier against germs.

The skin is not much more than a millimetre thick. Its top layer is always flaking off while new skin grows underneath. Although our skin is very thin, it covers a huge area. If a grown-up's skin could be stretched out in one piece, it would measure about 2 square metres and weigh about 3 kilogrammes!

Skin can be different colours because it has stuff called *pigment* in it. When we sunbathe, our skins go darker in colour. The amount of pigment increases. Dark-skinned people have more of this pigment than fair-skinned people.

Your brain tells the rest of the body what to do.

Your lungs take in clean air and push out used air.

Veins carry the used blood back to the heart.

Arteries are tubes that carry the blood from the heart.

Your heart pumps blood around your body.

Your stomach digests the food you eat.

# Staying Healthy

## Why does the doctor listen to your chest?

When you visit the doctor, he often wants to listen to your chest. He does this with an instrument called a *stethoscope*. One end of the stethoscope goes into the doctor's ears. He places the other end on your chest. Often he will ask you to take a deep breath while he listens.

The stethoscope is a bit like a microphone. It makes the sounds from your heart and lungs louder so that the doctor can hear them. By listening, the doctor can often tell whether there is anything wrong. If you have a bad cough, for instance, the doctor can tell how much fluid is blocking your lungs. He can then decide whether or not you need some medicine.

By using a stethoscope, the doctor can make sure your heart and lungs are working well.

## Why do we have to have injections?

When we are ill, the doctor often gives us medicine. It may be in the form of tablets or syrup. These take time to have an effect. But sometimes we must have medicine quickly, to cure a disease before it gets worse, or to stop pain. The doctor will then give an injection. The medicine is put into an instrument called a *hypodermic syringe* and is injected straight into the body – either directly into a blood vein or into muscle. The medicine can get to work straight away.

Left: this boy is having an injection.

Below: In hospital, most people stay in wards with other patients where doctors and nurses can look after them.

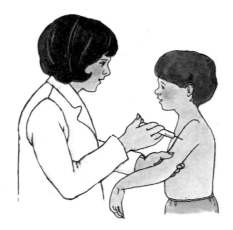

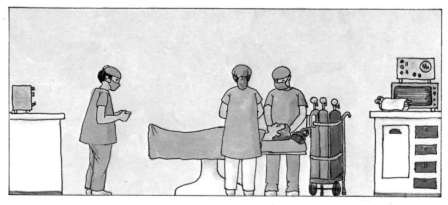

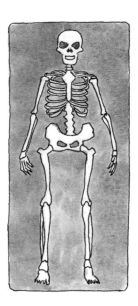

Above: Everything in the operating theatre must be kept as clean as possible. All the instruments are made extra clean by sterilization, and the doctors and nurses must wear special clothes and face masks so as to keep infection away from the patient.

Right: An X-ray picture of all your bones would look something like this. But X-ray photos are almost always just of one part of the body.

Below: Some people need special aids when they are ill or injured. Crutches help patients who cannot walk on both legs. Those who cannot walk at all get about in a wheelchair.

Bottom: People are helped to walk and move after illnesses or injuries.

Injections also protect people from disease. These injections are called *inoculations*. Today, most children in Western countries are inoculated against measles, whooping cough, diphtheria, and other diseases. The inoculation gives us a very mild form of the disease that we hardly notice. But this protects us from catching the proper disease later on.

### How do X-ray machines work?

X-ray machines can see inside your body. X-rays can go right through very thick substances. They can also make an impression on photographic film.

Doctors use X-rays to take photographs of the organs inside the body. The denser parts like bones show up well. If you have a broken arm, the X-ray machine will take a picture of the break in the bone. Then the doctor can see how bad it is and how to treat it. Other parts of the body do not show up so well. Then, doctors sometimes give a patient a "meal" of a special chemical. When the chemical reaches the part of the body doctors want to examine, they take an X-ray photo. The chemical helps those organs to show up more clearly.

# Games People Play

### Is karate just a sport?

Karate was invented by the Japanese. At first, karate was not a sport. It was a way of fighting without weapons. In karate many parts of the body are used to strike an opponent, including the head, knee, elbow or foot. People who practise karate are taught to aim quick, hard blows at weak points in their opponent's body. They learn self control. They wear special loose clothing and practise in bare feet.

Today karate is practised in most countries as a sport. Each player learns to respect his opponent's skill. No blows to the face or dangerous blows are allowed.

Above: Karate began in Japan as a system of self defence. Today it is a popular sport in many countries.

Below: Watersports can be fun for people of all ages. Many, such as swimming and sailing, are now Olympic sports.

Canoeing

Wind surfing

Sailing

Diving

Swimming

Water skiing

## What is the Tour de France?

Cycling has been a popular sport since the 1870s. The most famous and most difficult of all cycle races is the Tour de France, held in France since 1903. The contestants cover about 4480 kilometres in 25 days. People get very excited during the race and huge crowds turn out to watch it. The winner often becomes a national hero. Other countries have followed France's example. Today, Italy, Britain, Canada and Mexico all have touring races.

Cycle racing is now an outdoor and indoor sport and is included in the Olympic Games.

Association football is played in most parts of the world.

### The word "football" means different things to different people. How many kinds of football are there?

"Football" is any ball game in which the ball is kicked. In China people played a kind of football called *tsu-chu* as early as 1000 BC. Later, *tsu-chu* was used to train soldiers in the Chinese armies.

Today the best known kind is Association football, often called soccer. It is played in nearly all parts of the world. Teams from many countries compete for the World Cup. In soccer, two teams of players try to get a round ball into the opponent's goal. The players may touch the ball with any part of their body except hands and arms.

Rugby football and American football both use an oval ball that is pointed at each end. The players can throw, kick or run with the ball to get it over the opponent's goal line. Both these games are rougher than soccer, because players can tackle their opponents to try to get the ball. Players in American football games wear helmets, face guards and thick padding on their shoulders and legs.

211

### Where did the first Olympic Games take place?

The first Olympic Games were held at Olympia, in ancient Greece. They began as a religious festival to honour the Greek god Zeus. The early games included music and poetry as well as athletics. Events included a fourhorse chariot race, long jumping, throwing the discus and javelin, boxing and wrestling. About 1500 years later the Olympic Games were revived. The first modern Olympics took place in Athens in Greece in 1896.

Running

Bobsleigh racing

### How many Olympic sports are there?

When the first modern Olympic Games were held, only 12 countries took part. There were barely 300 athletes. By the 1960s there were 7500 athletes from 94 countries. The Olympics are held in a different host country every four years. There are about 20 different kinds of sport and about 200 events in all. Track and field sports have always been the most popular, but today many other sports such as boxing, fencing, rowing, football and hockey are included.

Winter sports such as skiing, tobogganing, skating, bobsleighing and ice hockey are part of the Winter Olympics, also held every four years. The 1980 Olympics were held in Moscow, while the Winter Olympics took place in Lake Placid, USA.

Basketball

## What is a puck?

A puck is a hard rubber disc used in ice hockey games. The players use hockey sticks to try to hit the puck into the opposing team's goal. Ice hockey is a very fast-moving sport. The players wear skates and race at high speeds across the ice. They must be expert skaters and be able to stop and turn quickly. All the players wear heavy pads to protect them from falls or collisions with other players.

Boxing

Tennis

## How old a sport is boxing?

People have always used their fists to fight. But what began as fighting soon turned into a sport. Boxing and wrestling were both sports as long as 5000 years ago. Pictures found in an ancient temple near Baghdad in Iraq show boxers with their hands bound in leather strips – the earliest boxing "gloves". Today, boxing follows rules drawn up by the Marquis of Queensberry in 1865.

Ice hockey

Goal

Goalie

Stick

Puck

# Rivers and Dams

## What makes rivers have bends?

Rivers help to shape the land. A young, fast-flowing river will carve a deep, steep-sided valley. A slice across one looks something like the letter V. Over thousands of years, a river carves a deep, broad valley from the land. The sides of the valley

A river flows fast where the land slopes steeply or where its channel narrows.

Where the land is flat and level, a river flows slowly, forming bends, or meanders.

become less steep. The river begins to wear away the softer banks to form bends, called *meanders*.

## Which is the left bank of a river?

The left bank of a river is the one on your left when you are facing the river's mouth, or *downstream*. The right bank is on your right.

A big river usually has smaller rivers or streams running into it. These are called *tributaries*.

## Where are there rivers of ice?

A great deal of the Earth's fresh water is frozen into ice. A huge ice cap covers the land round the South Pole. In some places the ice is 2500 metres thick.

In mountain areas, snow and ice cover the highest peaks and valleys all year round. Rivers of ice, called *glaciers*, form from thick layers of snow to fill many mountain valleys. Glaciers help to shape many mountains. The rocks stuck in the ice of a glacier wear away the walls and floor of the valley as the glacier slowly creeps downhill. A slice across one of these valleys would look something like the letter U.

Many valleys that are now ice-free were formed during the last Ice Age, which came to an end about 20,000 years ago. Then, ice covered much of Europe, Asia and North America. There were glaciers where London is now. And in some places the ice piled up more than a thousand metres high.

Glaciers are moving rivers of snow and ice. They move slowly, usually not more than a metre or so a day.

## What is an island

Islands are pieces of land entirely surrounded by water. The largest islands on Earth are Greenland, New Guinea and Borneo. Australia is looked upon as a continent, not an island.

Islands near the coast are often high pieces of land that are part of the mainland. The water round about them is not very deep. But some islands are in the middle of great oceans. They are usually the tops of huge volcanoes that have built up from the ocean floor. In warm seas, coral islands grow from the skeletons of thousands of tiny coral animals cemented together.

Islands can be either near the mainland or out in the middle of deep oceans. The Pacific Ocean contains about 20,000 islands.

## Why do we build dams?

Most dams are built to store water or to harness water power. In dry areas or in places where lots of water is needed to supply cities, rivers are dammed to form *reservoirs*. These are lakes that are made when the water held back by the dam floods the valley on either side of the river. The

Waterfalls are formed when rivers flow over hard rock and onto softer rock. As they wear the soft rock away, they must drop from the hard rock above to the softer rock below.

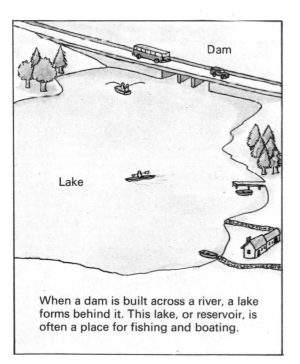

When a dam is built across a river, a lake forms behind it. This lake, or reservoir, is often a place for fishing and boating.

water in these reservoirs may be channeled to the places where it is needed or stored for use when other sources of water dry up.

Before the invention of electricity, rivers were dammed so that their flow could be controlled to turn waterwheels. People were using waterwheels to grind grain hundreds of years ago. Today, the falling water released from a dammed-up lake can be used to spin turbines that generate electric current. Electricity produced like this is called *hydroelectricity*.

# Land and Water

### Where does all the water finish up?

The big picture below shows how some of the things in the smaller pictures on the previous pages and here join together.

You can see how all the water from streams, rivers, snowy peaks, and glaciers ends up in the sea.

You can also see how the river was dammed to make a lake.

Some mountains are so high that snow stays on the top all year round. Hills are not as high as mountains.

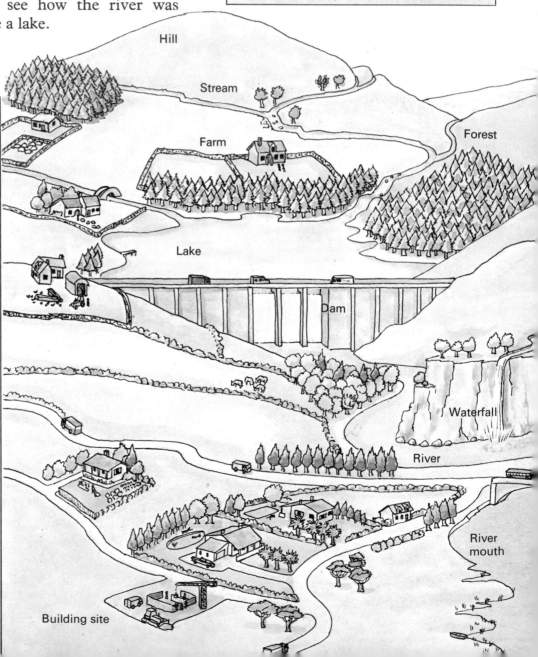

Hill

Stream

Farm

Forest

Lake

Dam

Waterfall

River

River mouth

Building site

## What is a harbour?

A harbour is an area of sheltered water where ships and boats can tie up safely. The harbour on the right has strong walls made of concrete. These walls keep out the waves which roll in from the sea. Harbour walls are called *breakwaters*.

Peak

Mountains

Glacier

Valley

Village

Orchard

Road

Cliff

Island

Beach

Town

Sea

Harbour

# The Same but Different

## When did people first use coins?

People all over the world use money. But the coins used in other countries are all quite different.

The first coins were used in Asia Minor about 700 years before the time of Christ. They were made of a mixture of gold and silver. These first coins were about the size and shape of a bean.

Can you find out where some of the coins below come from?

## When were the first stamps made?

People all post letters. But every country has its own stamps. Can you recognize which countries the ones in the picture below come from?

The first stamps came into use in Britain in the year 1840. They were a one-penny black and a two-penny blue. They had a picture of Queen Victoria on them, and the black one has become known as the "Penny Black". They had no perforations.

## THE CHINESE YEARS

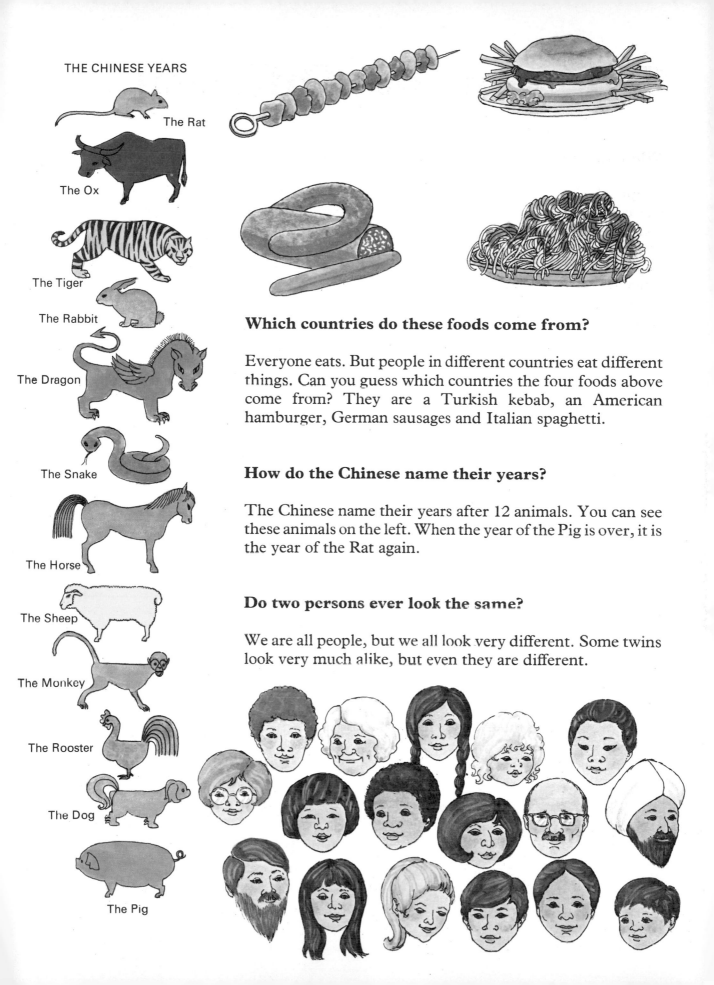

The Rat

The Ox

The Tiger

The Rabbit

The Dragon

The Snake

The Horse

The Sheep

The Monkey

The Rooster

The Dog

The Pig

## Which countries do these foods come from?

Everyone eats. But people in different countries eat different things. Can you guess which countries the four foods above come from? They are a Turkish kebab, an American hamburger, German sausages and Italian spaghetti.

## How do the Chinese name their years?

The Chinese name their years after 12 animals. You can see these animals on the left. When the year of the Pig is over, it is the year of the Rat again.

## Do two persons ever look the same?

We are all people, but we all look very different. Some twins look very much alike, but even they are different.

# INDEX